The House Witch

Your Complete Guide to

CREATING A MAGICAL SPACE WITH RITUALS AND SPELLS FOR HEARTH AND HOME

ARIN MURPHY-HISCOCK
AUTHOR OF *THE GREEN WITCH*

Adams Media
New York   Amsterdam/Antwerp   London   Toronto
Sydney/Melbourne   New Delhi

Adams Media
An Imprint of Simon & Schuster, LLC
100 Technology Center Drive
Stoughton, MA 02072

First Adams Media hardcover edition November 2018

ADAMS MEDIA and colophon are trademarks of Simon & Schuster.

For information about special discounts for bulk purchases, please contact Simon & Schuster Special Sales at 1-866-506-1949 or business@simonandschuster.com.

The Simon & Schuster Speakers Bureau can bring authors to your live event. For more information or to book an event contact the Simon & Schuster Speakers Bureau at 1-866-248-3049 or visit our website at www.simonspeakers.com.

Interior design by Michelle Kelly

Manufactured in China

20

Library of Congress Cataloging-in-Publication Data
Murphy-Hiscock, Arin, author.
The house witch / Arin Murphy-Hiscock, author of The Green Witch.
Avon, Massachusetts: Adams Media, 2018.
Includes bibliographical references and index.
LCCN 2018031985 | ISBN 9781507209462 (hc) | ISBN 9781507209479 (ebook)
Subjects: LCSH: Witchcraft. | Home--Miscellanea.
Classification: LCC BF1566 .M8835 2018 | DDC 133.4/3--dc23
LC record available at https://urldefense.proofpoint.com/v2/url?u=https-3A__lccn.loc
.gov_2018031985&d=DwIFAg&c=jGUuvAdBXp_VqQ6t0yah2g&r=eLFfdQgpHVW0iSAzG8F-WtSjrFv
CD9jGMJBHtzyExXhmHvwB7sjMCnFuKz95Uyqa&m=MJVMeOKlNhDzX_yizYEiCQmanHcnxiCkj
M89EcXeOgg&s=Kormv2caDLILE-FPMUlcHRuaAxG3vRxA9vHVn9GdZcY&e=

ISBN 978-1-5072-0946-2
ISBN 978-1-5072-0947-9 (ebook)

Dedication

For Ada and Audrey, who are discovering magic as a way to help the world around them and heal those they care about.

Acknowledgments

My endless thanks go out to the team at Simon & Schuster who worked on this book to bring it to a new round of readers, including Eileen Mullan and Brett Palana-Shanahan. Thanks also go out again to my original team at Adams Media who helped develop the first version of this book, especially Andrea Hakanson. Of all the paths within witchcraft, hearth magic is the one closest to my heart, and I will be forever grateful to her for helping me to initially share it with readers.

Contents

Introduction

Your home is a place of refuge, renewal, and creativity, where you begin and end each day. It is also the primary root of your energy and spirituality. The house witch works to honor and strengthen that sacred space, making it as simple, peaceful, and nourishing as possible.

Unlike green witches who focus on nature-based practices and kitchen witches who concentrate on food and cooking, the house witch explores and uses the magic of the home. While other spiritual paths often look *beyond* the home to focus on the natural world, the house witch creates a solid and supportive place to work from—a literal (and magical) home base.

In *The House Witch*, you'll explore the energies of hearth and home and learn how you can create a spiritual haven for yourself and your loved ones in today's busy world. Inside these pages you'll learn how to:

- Locate and enhance your home's spiritual hearth
- Perform rituals to protect and cleanse your home

- Build a kitchen shrine
- Prepare recipes that blend magic and food
- Master the secrets of the cauldron and the sacred flame
- Bring the ancient house witch practices into modern times
- Produce hearth-based arts and crafts

In essence, the role of the house witch is to serve as a facilitator for the spiritual well-being of herself, her family, and her welcomed guests. Her home is her temple, which she tends in order to keep energy flowing smoothly and freely, as well as to honor the principles she upholds. She seeks to support and nurture her family (and extended community) in both a spiritual and physical fashion. So if you are ready to explore the magic that may be found or created in your home and use it to better your life, then let's get started.

Chapter 1

A Place to Call Home

IF THERE'S SOMETHING ALL PEOPLE HAVE IN COMMON, it's the need for shelter, nourishment, and a place to call home. That place is somewhere to return to for refuge, renewal, relaxation, and rejuvenation. In this chapter you'll learn about the concept of home and its place in a spiritual life.

Spirituality comes from within, and the spiritual path or practice you choose gives it context. One of the most common of those contexts is the hearth, the spiritual center of the home. No matter what your current spiritual path is, rooting it in your hearth makes a lot of sense and can nourish the rest of your spiritual life.

Hearthcraft and Home-Based Spirituality

Hearthcraft is a spiritual path rooted in the belief that the home is a place of beauty, power, and protection, a place where people are nurtured and nourished on a spiritual basis as well as a physical and emotional basis. Hearthcraft describes the home-based portion of the spirituality associated with the path of the house witch. It is not kitchen witchcraft, although that can play a role within a house witch's practice. It is also not green witchcraft, although that, too, can influence and enrich a hearth- and home-based practice.

Hearthcraft argues that spirituality, like many other things, begins at home. It is not enough to attend an out-of-home spiritual gathering at specific intervals; the home itself is an essential element within a nourishing, vibrant, ongoing spiritual practice. Once upon a time organized religion was depended upon to be the source for spiritual fulfillment. With increasing dissatisfaction being felt within organized religious institutions, the relocation of the spiritual focus to the home, either as the central element or a supportive one, makes sense. Honoring the hearth means honoring your origins, where you come from each day, and where you return each night.

Why Hearthcraft?

The word *hearth* is of Old English origin meaning the floor around a fireplace or the lower part of a furnace where molten metal is collected during the smelting process. Throughout the ages the hearth has come to symbolize domestic comfort and the entire home, perceived as the heart or center of the living space. Therefore, someone who practices hearthcraft is someone whose spiritual practices revolve around the hearth and home, as symbolized by the fireplace and the fire that burns within it.

Perhaps a more familiar term, *kitchen witch* is used popularly to mean someone who practices magic through cooking, baking, and/or through everyday activity. Hearthcraft differentiates from kitchen witchcraft by primarily emphasizing the spiritual aspect that runs through the practice, as opposed to the primarily magical practice of the kitchen witch. There's more about kitchen witches later in this chapter.

Hearthcraft, like other aspects of the house witch's path and other forms of kitchen and green witchcraft, revolves around practicality, with little ritualistic guidelines or necessary formality. Here are some keywords to keep in mind when you think about hearthcraft:

- Simple
- Practical
- Family-related
- Domestic
- Everyday
- Household

Keep It Simple

The practices suggested in this book are based in simplicity. Here the word *ritual* doesn't mean something full-blown and complicated; instead, it means an intuitive ceremony or something set apart from everyday action by mindfulness and conscious intent. Also, the word *magic* means the conscious and directed attempt to effect change by combining and directing energy toward a positive goal. The rituals and magical workings included in this book are only guidelines to give you an idea of how you can structure your own hearth-based spiritual practice.

Why Hearthcraft Is So Special

Hearthcraft functions on a very basic truth:

Living your life is a spiritual act.

Having said that, it can be hard to isolate exactly what constitutes spirituality and, by extension, how to actively support it in the home.

What makes hearthcraft so special is that the principles of it dovetail—in fact, are—the things you do every day in your home. In essence, this book is designed to help you recognize those things and lend awareness to them so that you can appreciate them all the more. It also offers some ideas on how to enhance those everyday actions and objects in order to facilitate or deepen your experience.

What Is Spiritual to You?

Nurturing the spiritual element of the home is key to the path of the hearth-based house witch. How can you do this? The answer depends on how you define *spiritual*. You've already read some basic definitions, but what is crucial to this practice is defining the term for yourself. Think about these questions:

- What constitutes a spiritual experience for you?
- What are the characteristics of a sacred object?
- What elements of an action render it spiritual?

These are huge questions, and the answers will be different for every person who tries to answer them. Attempting to define *spiritual* can be challenging, frustrating, and faith-testing. You may not be able to say more than "I just know when something is spiritual," and that's fine. In essence when you recognize something as spiritual, you acknowledge that something about it moves you or touches you deeply in a very specific way, evoking certain feelings that may be indefinable.

Focus Your Practice

Once you know what kinds of things you find spiritual, or what kinds of events or actions evoke that response within yourself, then you may have some idea of where to focus in your practice of home-based spirituality and how to identify or establish everyday activities that can support your spirituality, recognizing and using these spiritual moments to reinforce your commitment to making the home a spiritual place. One method of doing this is to use these moments or activities as an opportunity to think about "important" things (not "important" as in balancing your checkbook or picking up groceries for dinner but as an issue related to your spirituality); an opportunity to send good thoughts out toward your family, friends, and community; an opportunity to practice a form of "walking meditation," where you perform a simple, ongoing action with a clear mind. Perhaps you take a moment to say a prayer or simply open your heart and talk to God in whatever form you envision the Divine, the universe, the spirit of love, or whoever you feel like talking to.

Maintaining healthy spirituality means keeping yourself relaxed, focused, and practicing *something*. It means keeping the lines of communication open between you and something greater than you. The term *practice* is often used to describe what one does in respect to one's spiritual path, and it means physically or intentionally acting upon a theory associated with the path. By actively seeking out or defining spiritual activity, you create the opportunity to develop a deeper connection with the world around you. (Chapter 2 explores sanctity in more depth, especially as it pertains to the home.)

Everyday Things Can Be Magical

There is always a sense that something that is simple cannot possibly be as effective or powerful or useful as something more complicated or difficult. This is an odd human perception. People love to complicate things, possibly in order to have a scapegoat available if they fail. "It was too difficult!" they can cry. Humankind seems to instinctively eschew responsibility. But taking responsibility for your spiritual practice, working from the heart of your home outward, is a step toward a more rewarding relationship with the world around you.

Everything is, or can be, a magical act. Stirring a pot of soup as you reheat it can be a magical act. So can wiping down the counter, washing the dishes, filling the kettle, and arranging your tea caddy. So how do you make these things magical? Not with secret words or arcane shapes drawn in the air. It isn't the addition of something that is necessary, so much as a recognition and acknowledgment of something that is already there.

How do you recognize the magic? Try these steps:

- **Live in the moment.** Being in the moment is harder to do than it sounds. It means not thinking about your next action or the one you just performed, not thinking about how you have to leave in half an hour to pick the kids up from practice or how you have to remember to buy milk on the way home. It means thinking about what you are doing this precise moment instead. Just be. Feel the weight of the jug in your hand; feel the weight shift as you tilt it to pour the milk; hear the sound of the liquid flowing into the glass.

- **Be aware of your intent.** Awareness is key to most magical working. While you are performing your action, make sure you have a clear expectation of the associated result or energy. Envisioning a clearly defined result is key to success.

- **Direct your energy properly.** Focus your will and allow it to fill the action you are performing. Poorly directed energy is wasted.

- **Focus on an action.** It may go without saying that there should be an action upon which to hang your magical work, but for the sake of clarity it's worth noting that it is better to focus on a single action rather than a series of actions. It is harder to maintain focus over a long period of time, especially if you must change actions along the way.

Remember, hearthcraft is about keeping things simple and focusing on the actual work you are doing in the home. If you feel you need to speak during a moment you define as spiritual or magical working, speak from the heart or use a short prayer or poem that you already know and can apply to several situations. (See Chapter 10 for suggestions about spoken magic and prayers.)

In essence, magic is the art of clearly focusing your will to help create a change or transition of some kind. If you're familiar with the contemporary practice of magic, particularly in conjunction with your spiritual practice, then you know that certain symbols or objects can help you focus and lend energy to help accomplish that change. If you're interested in this kind of work as a supplement to your spiritual practice, you should read a book specifically focusing on magic and spellwork, such as my book *Power Spellcraft for Life*. As this book focuses mainly on maintaining a home-based spiritual practice, there isn't a lot of magic-based work described here. It does include folk wisdom and home-based tradition, however, which some people may identify or define as magic.

Although many people use the terms *house* and *home* interchangeably, there is a difference between them, and each term is used to describe something specific in this book. *House* refers to the physical dwelling, the four walls and the roof over your head and the address and geographic location of your residence. *Home* refers to the energy entity created by that physical dwelling, the family that lives in it, and the identity that arises from the interaction between the two.

How does this all tie in to spirituality? Every moment is an opportunity to be in the now, to appreciate the moment and to make it magical. By doing this, you acknowledge that even the simplest of tasks informs your spirit and can nurture your soul. Allowing yourself to be in the moment illustrates how special you are. Life is made of many tiny moments strung together, after all. Opening yourself to the simplest of tasks and allowing them to inspire you with some insight or wisdom, or even a moment of peace, illustrates that the Divine can whisper to you in the oddest of unexpected places. Hearthcraft is about communing with the Divine through everyday tasks, not through complicated formal ritual.

Building Your Spiritual Headquarters

The hearth-based house witch seeks to create and maintain the best possible home atmosphere for family and friends, to support, fuel, and nourish them on both a physical and spiritual level.

A house is a neutral structure, and a home is a living, thriving place that is created by the actions and intentions of the people who live within that house. The home is a sanctuary, a place of security. It is defined by the people who live in it, is created by them, and is keyed to their energy. Energy defines the home in more than one way: it feeds and propels it spiritually and emotionally, but it is also invested in the form of money that sets it up and maintains it. Mortgage payments, rent, furnishings, consumables are all fueled by energy in the form of money, which is earned by an individual through work or other exchange of energy. Emotion, time, and money are all valid forms of energy that go into running a household and home.

The home is where you build a base or headquarters from which you may venture out into the world, and to which you may return at the end of the day. It is a place where you can be yourself, where you can relax and allow the energy you control so tightly outside its walls to flow freely in a protected space. It makes an excellent and very immediate base for a spiritual practice.

Denise Linn, author of *Sacred Space*, says, "Homes are symbolic representations of ourselves, and in fact in a deeper sense are extensions of ourselves." She is absolutely right. On an unconscious level, how you treat your living space can very often give insight into how you perceive yourself. On a more active level, by consciously controlling how you organize and decorate your living space, you can impact your sense of self as well and influence how you feel. Environment affects your emotional, physical, and mental functioning; it makes sense that it affects your spiritual well-being too.

For many of us it's important to have a room or defined space within the home that is exclusively ours: a bedroom, a corner, an office or reading room. What is often overlooked is a communal area that is equally invested in with conscious awareness and is cared for in the way a private or personal space would be. Communal spaces in a home, such as living rooms, family rooms, bathrooms, and kitchens, become an aggregate of the energy of all the people who use them and the activities that take place within them.

Rather than allowing the energy to form willy-nilly without any sort of conscious direction, and living with whatever the result is, it's wise to take it in hand and guide the energy signature identity. In the next chapter, we'll explore the idea of how this impacts the spiritual health and well-being of the members of the family as well.

Energy is fluid and always moving, so the result is never permanent. Ongoing maintenance is ideal. And it's never too late to begin or to work to reverse the energy signature of a communal room that is unwelcoming or uncomfortable in some way.

Maintaining, guiding, and shaping the energy of a communal room is a form of caring for the health and well-being of the people who use it.

Caring for Those Inside Your Home

The practice of hearthcraft presupposes someone to care for, even if it is only yourself or your pets. Family is one of the cornerstones of hearthcraft.

Members of the family (and/or the residents of the home) are active participants in shaping and affecting the energy of the home. They maintain and continually nourish the spiritual element of the home by being active, communicative, loving, and physically present. They provide energy for the house witch to manage, which is one of the reasons for the practice. The living energy is important to the path. Without it, the home becomes more of a house.

The active, fluid, ever-changing dynamic of family ensures input and activity, essential elements of the spiritual well-being of a home. It is also important to remember that the family's interaction and support go beyond maintaining the general identity of the home, however: the family supports itself as individuals as well.

Think about Your Values

Increasingly, people are no longer members of a defined religious group, and thus it falls to the family to engage in spiritual support. This can be challenging, especially when you think about all the morals, ethics, and values that an organized religion defines and instills in its adherents. These three terms are slippery and sometimes are confused.

- **Morals:** standards of behavior or principles of right and wrong.
- **Ethics:** the moral principles governing or influencing conduct.
- **Values:** principles or standards of behavior. *Value (singular):* the regard that something is held to deserve; importance or worth.

Because these three definitions are so closely intertwined, let's simplify them:

- Morals are the principles of right and wrong.
- Ethics are the application of morals to one's behavior.
- Values are morals and ethics that an individual or society as a whole considers important and worthy of upholding.

Define what morals are important to you and actively demonstrate them through ethical behavior, especially at the hearth.

If your family is open to discussing spirituality, ask them for their input as well as you define the fundamental values you wish to associate with your hearth. It is only fair to include them and their beliefs, as what goes on at the hearth and in the home impacts and affects them as well. It can be quite illuminating to learn what morals and ethics your partner or children value, and they may surprise you by listing principles that you hadn't initially thought of.

Define Your Values

Here's an exercise you can engage in with your family or alone if you live by yourself. With your family, have a brainstorming session in which you talk about morals, ethics, and values, and make an overall list. Once the session is over, schedule another meeting for a couple of days later. Discuss the overall list that was created during the brainstorming session. From the global list, write down the issues that mean the most to the family. Put it on the fridge or pin it to a bulletin board so everyone can see it on a regular basis. For each item on the list, come up with a real-life example. For example, if one of the values is "eco-awareness," an example might be "taking lunch to work in a reusable lunch bag or bento box." An illustration for "compassion" might be "making someone a cup of tea and sitting down with them to show that someone cares about them."

Looking up each word on the list in the dictionary and reading out the definition may be illuminating as well, because the popular idea of the meaning of terms like *compassion* and *generosity* may not be what those terms actually mean. The family might discuss the difference between the dictionary definition and their understanding of the term and choose one meaning over the other if it bears more ethical weight with them and has a more positive influence on the way they wish to live their lives.

Caring for Those Outside Your Home

One of the essential elements of the hearthcraft path is a presupposition of a community of some kind to care for, whether it be yourself and a pet, your family, or your circle of friends. Most hearth-based house witches gravitate to the path because they feel the need to care for and nurture those who are close to them. A kitchen and a home are places where living people operate and interact. These people are literally the soul of the home, much as the hearth and fireplace are the heart of the house. As a result, the hearth-based house witch and her work can have a significant impact on her family and extended community as they interact within her sphere. The energy you maintain in your home will affect them, just as the energy they bring to your spiritual hearth will help to fuel it.

Hearthcraft posits a certain connection to community. The term *community* can sometimes be misleading, because we often associate it with a collection of people at large from a general area. The term can comprise any collection of people who are associated in pursuit of a similar goal.

Blood isn't the only indicator of close ties. The term *kin* is sometimes employed to describe those who are members of your blood family unit, but the term *akin* means something or someone essentially similar. People who have interests or philosophies akin to yours, with whom you have a spark of connection, and whom you invite into your home constitute a community of sorts as well. You may have close friends who hold special places in your heart, like-minded individuals who support and love you. In essence, they are family without the blood or legal ties.

Chosen family is the term often used to describe this circle. Chosen family is one such example of a close circle or community for whom your hearthcraft practices resonate in some way, whether they consciously know of your spiritual focus or not. Caring for them in emotional and physical ways—the supportive phone call, the cup of tea, the casserole in times of stress—is another way in which hearthcraft expresses itself. Caring for family and community to foster an environment that supports healthy growth and development at all levels is one of the things a house witch does.

The Path of Nurturing and Nourishing

The path of the house witch is rooted in the parallel paths of nurturing and nourishing. What do these words mean? The *Oxford English Dictionary* defines *to nurture* as "[to] rear and encourage the development of (a child); [to] cherish (a hope, belief, or ambition)." The noun is defined as "the action or process of nurturing; upbringing, education, and environment as a factor determining personality." It defines *to nourish* as to "provide with the food or other substances necessary for growth and health; [to] keep (a feeling or belief) in one's mind for a long time."

These two definitions describe a lot of hearthcraft in a nutshell: providing both physical and environmental sustenance in order to support growth, health, and development. Hearthcraft seeks to nourish and nurture on a spiritual level as well as the physical level. Let's explore why the basics of caring for someone are so important.

The Power of Basic Needs

Food and shelter are two of the most basic things an individual requires in order to live a good life. The concept of hearth and home reflects both of these things: warmth, protection, and food. These may seem to be insignificant when compared to other, more lofty goals in life, but in reality, these basic needs have to be fulfilled in order for you to explore the higher potential of your life and spirit.

Abraham Maslow's hierarchy of needs demonstrates this requirement. Maslow proposed a chain of needs, each rooted in the previous one. The hierarchy of needs demonstrates that fundamental physical requirements such as food, shelter, and protection are valid needs that must be addressed in order to create the security and energy required to pursue the other higher needs that Maslow outlined, such as creating an aesthetically pleasing environment or pursuing understanding of the self within the community. Maslow's theory isn't absolute, but it does provide a useful explanation for humanity's focus on the concept of hearth and home, and why it seems to be so ingrained in our cultures and psyches.

Maslow's hierarchy is often expressed as a pyramid with basic, or lower-order, needs at the bottom and higher-order needs at the top:

1. Basic physical needs, such as food and shelter.
2. Safety needs, such as protection from the elements and a feeling of security from the unknown.
3. The need for love and belonging, within a small social unit and a larger community.

4. Self-esteem needs, or confirming the sense of acceptance within the community, from which issues the sense of self-worth.
5. The need for understanding, again from the community within which one operates.
6. Aesthetic needs, or being able to manipulate one's environment in a desired way to reflect beauty or another value.
7. The need for self-actualization, which can be interpreted as self-improvement and feeling rewarded or satisfied by your life, as well as having the impetus to strive for more.
8. Transcendence and peak experience, the culmination of the process of self-actualization and the ultimate spiritual escape from the material world: the absence of need.

Hearthcraft tends to focus on securing and maintaining the basic needs. This is far from being simplistic or primitive: every person requires at least the first two needs of food and protection in order to survive. Hearthcraft is rooted in these primary needs, making it a necessary and highly respected path. Without the assurance of these basic needs, you cannot go on to explore more exalted paths or seek more challenging paths in life. In the end, the focal issues addressed in hearthcraft are required by every person in some way, shape, or form.

Knowing this, it is still hard to believe that there are people who dismiss the idea that anyone who works to maintain a secure and happy home is missing something or limiting themselves in some way. The casual dismissal of men or women who have chosen to follow a domestic-centered path as second-class citizens, for example, is shameful when one looks at cultural mores and stories that describe the woman as queen within her home, who managed and ordered and made sure the family had a safe, warm, secure, and successful base from which to operate, thereby maximizing their chances of success in their chosen paths. With basic needs met and accounted for, you can focus your energy on the higher, more spiritual needs, such as self-actualization and transcendence.

Practicing hearthcraft is an excellent method whereby confidence and self-esteem may be secured through answering basic needs. The more control you have over the energy and function of your home environment, the more likely you and your family are to be relaxed and happy. When you are relaxed, there are fewer obstacles to divert the life-renewing energy flowing through your life. Stress, anxiety, and fear commonly snarl up and divert the energy flowing through your life. Keeping a welcoming, serene, and happy hearth maximizes your potential to create a successful life, resting upon the firm foundation built at the hearth, in the spiritual heart of the home.

Kitchen Witchcraft

There are many other traditions that possess an element of hearthcraft to them, but the most familiar of them is likely to be kitchen witchcraft. As previously mentioned, the two paths are differentiated by emphasizing the spiritual element found in the path of the house witch, as opposed to the more magic-based path of the kitchen witch.

A kitchen witch is someone who practices magic through cooking, baking, and other kitchen-based activity. Patricia Telesco, arguably kitchen witchery's most visible practitioner, says in her book *A Kitchen Witch's Cookbook*, "Since we all have to prepare food at one time or another, why not make the best possible use of that time in the kitchen?"

The Kitchen Witch As Good Luck

The kitchen witch is also familiar for the use of her figure as a kitchen icon or good luck charm. Regardless of the spiritual path followed by the family, many homes feature a small witch doll, usually astride a broom, hanging somewhere in the kitchen. This little talisman is said to bring successful cooking and good luck to the residents of and visitors to the kitchen. Perhaps more precisely, such dolls are said to guard against failed cooking or cooking disasters. German folklore has it that they guard specifically against dough failing to rise, milk curdling, and fallen cakes. The dolls are made of many different materials. Some are corn husk dolls; some have dried apples for heads; others are made entirely of fabric. The earliest appearances of these kitchen icons are in German and Scandinavian traditions.

There are other parallels to the kitchen witch doll. As a harvest custom, communities in Britain and Europe would tie together the last sheaf of wheat and keep it over the winter as good luck and protection. Sometimes the sheaf was draped with cloth or otherwise dressed and adorned. Other communities would weave the first or last stalks cut in the harvest into various shapes of different sizes, including geometric shapes and animal forms. Confusingly, these were also called corn dollies, even when they were not in human form. The term *dolly* is thought to be derived from the word *idol*. These customs stemmed from the belief that the first or last stalks of wheat that were cut contained the spirit of the crop. By keeping the dolly in a place of honor and safety over the winter, the farmers would in essence be protecting the success of the next year's crops. The dolly was often plowed into the fields when the time came to prepare them for the spring planting, or it was burned after the harvest as an offering to the harvest deities. Sometimes the sheaf is referred to as the harvest queen, the corn mother, or the corn maiden, and there are a wide variety of shapes into which the stalks are woven, according to local tradition. The art is still practiced today and is called both corn dolly plaiting and wheat weaving. Beautiful abstract shapes and designs are created, as well as figures and religious objects.

If you wish to make your own protective kitchen witch icon, a craft detailing how to make a corn husk doll can be found in Chapter 10. Making a new one every year is certainly a possibility, after disposing of the old one by burning or shredding it and mixing it into your compost or mulch. It's a nice tradition to link to Thanksgiving, the autumnal equinox, or any of the harvest festivals found in various religious calendars. It may also be tied into a purification ritual, with the dismantling of the old, symbolizing the clearing of accumulated negativity or stale energy, and the introduction of the new, symbolizing a fresh start.

Chapter 2

Your Home As a Sacred Space

IT IS IMPORTANT TO REMEMBER that in hearthcraft the areas, actions, and times you hold sacred are not isolated from the everyday world; they are very much a part of it, and they lend their sanctity to what and who interacts with them. In other words, *we are blessed by interacting with what we consider sacred.* This is one of the most important precepts of home-based spirituality: by caring for and maintaining your home, you simultaneously enhance its sanctity while it touches and blesses you.

What Does It Mean to Be Sacred?

The central concept of hearth- and home-based spirituality puts forth that the home is sacred. But what does *sacred* really mean? *Sacer,* the Latin root of the term, means "holy." The

Oxford English Dictionary defines *sacred* as "connected with a deity and so deserving veneration; holy." Alternatively, it may mean "religious rather than secular." In plainer terms, it means that if something is considered sacred it is recognized as being touched by the realm of the gods in some way and is therefore something worthy of respect or honor. It is theoretically no longer of this world: it is set apart and revered or honored for this reason. Note that "set apart" does not mean isolated and worshipped. Instead, it means given honor within the context of the everyday world.

Sacred space, then, is a zone where you can touch the Divine, communicate with it, interact with it, or be influenced by it in a way that is clearer (or more easily perceived or felt) than in other places. We generally recognize certain sites as sacred: sites of grave tragedy, such as Auschwitz; sites of great beauty; sites consecrated to a particular religion, such as Chartres Cathedral or the Taj Mahal; sites that are historically significant, such as where peace treaties were signed, battles fought, and great people met; sites of commemoration, such as cemeteries and burial grounds; and sites of ancient activity, such as Stonehenge. Part of the mystery of sacred space is how it is familiar, and yet we can sense that there is something "other" about it. This tension is part of what we recognize when we sense that a place or object is sacred.

To consecrate something means to ritually designate it as sacred. While this action is found in many alternative spiritual paths as well as formal religions, it doesn't figure largely in hearthcraft. This is mainly due to the recognition that there is a touch of the sacred in all things, and the hearth is especially sacred due to its function.

There is no need to formally consecrate the hearth, because it is already sacred.

The Sanctity of Home

You guard your home; you defend it from unwanted intruders, both physical and otherwise. You invest great amounts of money in it, whether you rent or own it. You decorate it in a way that soothes you, or enlivens you, or reflects you in some way. Inviting someone into your home is a great concession. It says, "I trust you" in some way. You trust a guest to behave well, to be considerate, and to appreciate the personal space that is yours.

Respecting the Home

The Japanese culture demonstrates how highly it respects the sanctity of the home by having people remove their shoes before entering a dwelling. It shows respect for the hosts by abstaining from ruining the floor covering (usually called a *tatami*—a woven-plant fiber-like straw that is easily damaged by footwear), as well as avoiding tracking dirt into the home. Symbolically, removing the footwear also represents leaving the worries and problems experienced outside at the door.

To define the space between the outside world and the private space of the home, there is an entryway referred to as the *genkan*, where the footwear is removed and stored in a cupboard or shelf divided into a series of cubes called a *getabako*. The *genkan* functions as a buffer between the sacred space of the private home and the uncontrolled outside world. The level of the actual living space is usually one step up from the entryway, and this step functions as another kind of buffer, requiring you to physically step up and away from both the outside world and the transitional area. There is an entire etiquette associated with the *genkan* and how shoes are removed and placed, and how to enter the home as well. Japan isn't the only culture to employ this custom. Parts of Korea, China, Indochina, and Southeast Asia also have customs involving the removal of footwear before entering sacred places.

> In Japan, footwear is removed before entering shrines, temples, and some restaurants. Many homes provide slippers for visitors to wear once they have removed their outdoor footwear. A different pair of slippers is worn in the bathroom and is not to be worn outside it, further demonstrating how the different energies of the home are kept as separate as possible.

The custom of removing one's hat before entering a home is also associated with respect. In Western culture, hats are removed to demonstrate respect for a person, a place, or an action, or to illustrate recognition of one's humbler station. Hats are removed by men in a Christian church to humble oneself before God; however, some sects require that women cover their heads before entering the church. Hats are generally worn outdoors, and to wear one inside smacks of poor breeding as well as disrespect for the sanctity of the place. Conversely, Judaism instructs its adherents to always cover their heads in a temple, usually with a brimless cap called a *kippah* or *yarmulke*.

Sacred Spaces

The home is set apart as sacred space, separate from the outside world. Within the home there are further zones of sacred space, the hearth being the zone this book will focus on. Sacred spaces are recognized by our deference to them and defense of them: they are sacred to us. Some spaces are recognizable by other people as sacred: the collection of family portraits on a shelf, for example, or a collection of statuary. Sacred things have a certain aura to them, and we are both drawn to them and understand innately that we ought not to touch or interfere with them. This aura can originate from the item itself, which may have drawn you to acquire it in the first place, or it may be instilled in it by your designation of it as sacred. The former may have come about by the item's previous associations or its origins.

There are sacred spaces that are almost universally recognized, and sacred spaces that are unique to one or a small group of individuals. Something can very well be sacred to you and no one else, and that's fine. A space or object does not have to be validated as sacred by anyone else for it to have power for you. While you may not sense the sanctity of a place or item held sacred by someone else, it is always courteous to respect the other person's sense of sanctity.

The Sacred Hearth

The hearth symbolizes sacred space wherein you can be yourself, where you are secure, where you can be open. The hearth is a wellspring, a place where people can recharge, where they can go for comfort on a basic level. It is a place where you can access energy, wisdom, and power more easily than anywhere else within your home—and outside it, for that matter. It is a place where you can explore your thoughts and feelings, a place of communion with family and the Divine, a place where you can stand to direct that energy, wisdom, and power to a greater good on a family level and the level of your community. The hearth is a place of power.

When people use the term *hearth*, it generally evokes a vague idea of a symbol in the form of a fireplace of some kind. People who possess a fireplace or know a bit about history may be able to identify it specifically as part of the fireplace layout. Since the word is central to this book, let's take a moment to explore the various definitions of what a hearth is.

Hearth is usually defined as the brick- or stone-lined space at the base of a chimney where a fire can be built and at which cooking takes place; the stone- or brick-paved, tiled, or otherwise protected area next to or surrounding a fireplace that extends out into the room; the likewise paved flat surface on which a stove sits (especially an iron wood-burning stove); and the figurative home built around the fireplace as symbolic center.

Here's an interesting fact for you. The term *focus* (plural: *foci*) is a Latin word meaning "hearth, fireplace; fire, flame; center; or central point." How appropriate, then, that the hearth is considered the focus of home-based spirituality.

As an extension of the fireplace, the hearth is a natural place to gather. In older times, the fireside was a place where chores were done—sometimes out of necessity if the fire was an essential part of the task—for light, warmth, or comfort. It was a social place as well as a place to work. Soap-making, candle-making, and dyeing all require heat and water when done by hand, for example. Caring for the young, the elderly, or the ill would also have been done near the fire for its light and warmth. The hearth was centrally located in most homes, making it a natural gathering place for social reasons as well as practical ones. Lessons and teaching would also take place by the hearth. In short, the hearth has always been a very active zone of the kitchen area and of the home overall.

The Hearth Fire

The home is recognized as being sacred, set apart from the outside world. Within this zone there is a further sacred zone: the hearth, the location of the central fire of a home. In essence, the fireplace functioning as a symbolic center of a home exemplifies the concept of the hearth as a sacred fire.

Fire is seen as sacred in many cultures. Remember, the definition of *sacred* is something recognized as being touched by the realm of the gods in some way and therefore something worthy of respect or honor. So, the hearth fire as something sacred means it is a place where the spiritual world intersects with the everyday world: it is a place or object through which communication can take place.

Why is fire considered sacred? Fire is a symbol of vitality, for it "lives," "eats," and "breathes." When it burns, it symbolizes the spark of life that animates us. Fire is one of the four physical elements the ancients recognized as the building blocks of the world. It is recognized as being alive more than the other three elements due to its nature: it appears to have a mind of its own, it eats, it sleeps, it dies. Humankind must respect both its useful properties and its destructive properties as well: fire destroys indiscriminately, with rage and a primal fury that we can only attempt to control; however, that destruction very often purifies in preparation for regrowth and new creations.

Fire has played an important role in religion. The symbol of the eternal flame is a common concept in several religions; it has also been used to symbolize the presence of the Divine. In Christian myth, for example, God manifested as a burning bush; the sanctity of the flame was demonstrated by the fact that it did not consume the bush as fuel. Fire is also a method by which offerings are made, as well as a method of divination.

Fire is a symbol of spiritual energy, as is the sun, and indeed shares many traits and energies with the solar luminary. As a spiritual symbol, fire illuminates personal/emotional/spiritual darkness, which may be why so many religions use candles and oil-based flames as part of their tools and accoutrements. Candles are frequently used to symbolize energy of all kinds, activity, illumination, and faith, among other things.

The Role of the Hearth Fire at Home

In times past, fire played an important role in the home. It was a source of light and warmth, and it cooked food. Starting a fire was a time-consuming task, and so the hearth fire was banked at night to keep the coals and embers alive in order to use it as a basis for the next day's fire. The kitchen fire was so crucial to daily life that to allow it to go out demonstrated unpreparedness. It was a sacred task of sorts to conscientiously think ahead and to maintain a basic supply of fuel, in order to keep the house in order and running smoothly. The absence of a fire, whether through negligence or otherwise, meant the lack of warmth, the lack of a method to cook nourishing food, a lack of protection, and so forth.

In Ireland, the only time the household fire was intentionally allowed to go out was at Beltaine, the festival that modern spiritual paths place at the beginning of May. A main fire was lit at Tara, the spiritual center of Ireland, by the king or the druids, and from this fire all the other household fires were symbolically relit. This practice demonstrated unity throughout the kingdom as well as recognizing the spiritual power of the monarch or the druids.

Fuel for the fire is as important as the fire itself. Oil in particular serves as the fuel for many spiritually symbolic flames. Oil was (and is now again becoming) a precious commodity. Generally extracted from plant matter, it was so valuable that it was used as an offering to deities and as gifts to churches and temples. You can make a similar offering by giving a thimbleful of oil to your hearth spirits on a regular basis at a schedule of your choosing. In

Chapters 3 and 6 you'll find other ideas for incorporating an oil lamp into your spiritual practice.

Building a Needfire

The sacred fire also manifested in the form of bonfires, sometimes called needfires. The needfire was a custom by which a bonfire was kindled for a specific spiritual purpose. The exact purpose depends on which culture is kindling the fire. Some of these fires were required to be lit by the friction method (rubbing two sticks together or some variation thereof); others required a certain number of people to build them, or a certain combination of woods, or to be lit at a certain time of day. Often, the bonfire had to be the only fire burning within a certain distance; if another flame burned within its specified boundary, the power of the needfire would be rendered ineffective. Sometimes, this bonfire would serve as the source from which all the previously extinguished home fires were relit, or to produce smoke through which cattle or other livestock would be driven in order to protect them from illness. The practice of building and lighting a needfire or bonfire underlines the folk belief in the ability of fire to purify or bless, an extension of its innate sanctity.

Making a Cauldron-Based Needfire

Not everyone has the acreage or the fuel (or can obtain a permit) to build an outdoor bonfire. As most modern homes don't have a fireplace, and many towns have bylaws about building a fire in your backyard (if you have one), this is an excellent way to create a small, time-defined sacred fire.

Make sure your cauldron will be strong enough to withstand intense heat. If your cauldron, or the vessel you use as a cauldron, is not made of cast iron or a material designed to withstand intense heat, do not use it for this task. The heat will cause materials such as ceramics or glass to shatter. If you have a fireplace, you can put your cauldron on the hearth while you burn the needfire. Otherwise, place a heatproof trivet, pad, or stone under the cauldron and make sure the cauldron sits securely on it. Never put the cauldron on a wooden or fabric-covered surface.

While rubbing alcohol is specified in the following list of supplies because it is inexpensive and easily found, you can use any high-percentage alcohol available in liquor stores, such as ethanol (grain alcohol, such as Everclear) or liquors like vodka or brandy. These make lovely offerings to a deity or spirit. Remember, the higher the percentage of alcohol in the liquor, the hotter the fire, so plan accordingly. Make sure your room is ventilated; while this fire does not produce toxic gases or smoke, it does get very, very hot.

You will need:

- Epsom salts
- Rubbing alcohol
- Blend of herbs and resins (your choice)
- Heatproof trivet or pad, or a flat stone
- Long-handled match

- Large bag of sand or earth
- Lid for the cauldron (make sure it is heavy)
- Fire extinguisher (CO_2 or dry chemical)

1. Measure out equal parts of Epsom salts and alcohol. Place the salts in the bottom of the cauldron and pour the alcohol over them.

2. Pour the herbal mixture into the cauldron. Place the cauldron on the heatproof trivet or stone.

3. Light the long-handled match and touch it to the mixture. It will burst into almost silent flame, the tops of the flames leaping above the cauldron. The fire will burn until the alcohol has been consumed. Throughout the fire, but more so when the flames begin to die away, you will hear tiny pops and sizzles as the salt cracks in the heat and the herbs and resins are consumed by the flames.

4. Do not even think about adding more alcohol into the cauldron while the flames are burning! Keep the alcohol/salt proportion equal until you are confident about handling the resulting fire; then and only then may you tweak the proportions. Never pour a large amount of alcohol over the salts; the resulting flames can be several feet high and can cause major damage to you or your house. Be safe and use common sense.

5. The fire will die away within a few minutes, but keep your sand, lid, and fire extinguisher handy in case you need them to put out the fire.

I cannot stress how dangerous this activity can be if you do not approach it with respect and common sense. There is a reason the last three items are on the supply list: the heavy lid is to smother the flames if they get out of hand, and the bag of sand or earth is to pour over the fire if you need to douse it immediately. The suggested fire extinguisher is there as further backup. Do not leap over this fire or ever leave it unattended. Also watch your sleeves and hair, and make sure you set the cauldron away from anything flammable, such as curtains.

The Epsom salts soak up some of the alcohol and keep the fire burning in a more stable fashion. The flames will consume the herbs and resins you added, making this a lovely way to make an offering or to cleanse a room. This is also a wonderful way to scry (which means to perceive by gazing into something) or meditate by watching the flames. The fire dies away within a handful of minutes, depending on how much alcohol is in the cauldron.

Note: Instead of adding herbs directly to the salt, you can steep your selected herbs or flowers in the alcohol you plan to use. Steep them for at least 2 weeks, then strain and bottle the alcohol. Label it clearly and do not use it for any other purpose.

Smooring/Banking Your Fire

Smooring is a term encountered often in Celtic prayer, and it means banking a fire. In this modern age even the phrase "banking a fire" may be mysterious. From the context in which it's generally found, one can infer that it is something done to preserve a fire in some way so that it may be revived the next morning. And it's almost that simple. To bank a fire literally means to build up a protective wall of ashes or stones around the coals in order to keep it from spreading dangerously while you sleep, and to protect it from drafts and disturbances. By protecting the coals in this way, they can be used as the basis for building a new fire the next day. If the fire is outdoors and you intend to use it for more than one day, you can plan to build it next to a rock or dirt wall to help shelter it in this way. A fire ring or pit at a campground is basically this sort of design.

The word *bank* when used as a verb means to "heap or form into a mass or mound," and that's precisely what's done to bank a fire. You don't cover the coals or embers entirely; that would smother them and have the opposite effect of what you're intending. Scrape the coals and embers together, then scrape the ashes up around them, insulating them. If you need more insulation, use rocks. If you're banking in a fireplace, close the flue and the fire doors, if you have them.

Since most people have electricity to provide light and heat, smooring is a skill and a practice that has generally fallen out of use. In a spiritual context, however, it provides an opportunity to gather yourself back into yourself, in a manner of speaking, to pull your energy back from all the different directions in which the day has scattered it. In essence, it's a moment of personal reconnection with the self. You can think of it as banking your personal flame, if you like, caring for it in such a way that it is sheltered and protected overnight and ready for use the next day.

Bank Your Inner Flame

Do this after you have finished cleaning up and just before you head to bed. You can try doing it before and after you prepare yourself for bed; one way may be more useful for you and provide a better effect. The goal is to evaluate the day without judgment. You can do this in the kitchen or anywhere else in your home. If the weather is good you may wish to do it outside on the back porch or steps.

1. Stand or sit with a relaxed frame. If you know a relaxation exercise, run through it to rid yourself of any excess stress and tension in your body.

2. Think back to how you felt when you woke up, and then think back over your day's activities. Take note of how they made you feel: happy, angry, frustrated, sad, or peaceful. Remember, this retrospective isn't done with the intent to judge how you handled yourself, simply to accept the day as it was and yourself as you are. This doesn't have to be a long step; you don't have to think through every event in detail. Call them up as impressions.

3. When you have finished thinking back over the day, close your eyes and take three slow, deep breaths. As you exhale each breath, allow any fear or worry or irritation connected with the day to flow out of you.

4. Feel yourself here, now, at this moment, and accept yourself. If you like, at this point you may say a brief prayer or a simple phrase, such as *I accept myself. Watch over me as I sleep, spirits of the hearth, and guard my loved ones and our home. I bid you good night.*

5. As the final act, do something physical and symbolic of finishing the day. You could turn off the light (be it the kitchen light or

wherever you are) or close the door if you have been outside or standing at the door. If you have been sitting with a candle, using the flame as a meditative and calming focus, snuff it out by blowing it out, pinching it, or using a candle snuffer.

If you like, you can say a prayer in place of the previous phrase. You may already have a prayer that fits the purpose, or you may wish to write a new one. Saying a prayer that offers you an opportunity to connect with the Divine or the spirits of your hearth affirms your connection to it or them.

This is the traditional smooring prayer used in the Highlands of Scotland, as collected by Alexander Carmichael in the *Carmina Gadelica*. It calls on both Mary and Brigid (invoked here as Bride, a Scottish version of the name) as deities of domestic life to bless the home and the inhabitants. If you like, you can substitute other deity names or simply use the term "the Divine" to encompass your concept of God. The original prayer reads as follows:

I will smoor the hearth
As Mary would smoor;
The encompassment of Bride and of Mary,
On the fire and on the floor,
And on the household all.
Who is on the lawn without?
Fairest Mary and her Son,
The mouth of God ordained, the angel of God spoke;
Angels of promise watching the hearth,
Till white day comes to the fire.

Chapter 3

Your Spiritual Hearth

HEARTHCRAFT RECOGNIZES that your home is a sacred place, a place that has the power to refresh you, relax you, and rejuvenate you. But how precisely can you intentionally tap into this power? This chapter explores methods you can use to locate, bless, and work with your spiritual hearth in your home and in yourself.

Locating Your Spiritual Hearth

The spiritual hearth represents a refuge from the outside world, as well as a sacred place designed to maximize spiritual benefit. Deliberately designing a place of beauty, a place of serenity and calm, can be a challenge. First of all, you'll have to deal with the physical limitations or drawbacks of the building in which you're living. You'll also have to deal with the needs and preferences of the other people who live in your house and your budget. Making the most of what you have is part of the practical aspect of hearthcraft. This is one of the main reasons the spiritual hearth revolves around the energy and atmosphere of the home, both of which can be cultivated by behavior, attitude, and positive outlook, rather than by physical rearranging or redecorating. Although the latter can certainly enhance your home and the effect you are seeking to achieve, it's important to remember that the spiritual hearth functions on the level of energy and spiritual benefit.

The spiritual hearth is the symbolic heart of your home. Although the kitchen seems to be the logical modern parallel of the physical hearth, it doesn't necessarily have to be the spiritual hearth of your home. Many people have to live with kitchens that are poorly laid out, seemingly afterthoughts of the architect. A kitchen that is cramped or unwelcoming is very definitely not the symbolic heart of your home. If this is the case with you, think about how the areas of your home are used and where people seem to gravitate, to help you determine where the symbolic heart of your home is. Perhaps everyone brings their various activities into the living room or dining room or family room. Perhaps the curve of a staircase where there is a window overlooking the garden is where people pause. Or perhaps the spiritual center of your home is where you can feel the rest of it around you, even if the physical center is in a hallway or an odd spot.

If you can't put your finger on the heart of your home, and you do not wish to designate your kitchen as the symbolic hearth, then consciously choose another area. If you have a fireplace, this makes an excellent physical representation of the spiritual hearth, provided it is in a room that sees frequent use. There is no point to establishing a symbolic hearth in an unused fireplace located in a room that people avoid.

Blessing the Hearth

Once you have determined or chosen the heart of your home and designated it as the physical location to represent the spiritual hearth, you can perform a purification and blessing (see Chapter 7) or the ritual to recognize the sanctity of the hearth that is found later in this chapter.

This physical representation of the spiritual hearth can be used as a location to focus your spiritual activity. You may wish to create an altar or a shrine there, or use it as a place to meditate or pray. You may want to stand there when you wish to draw strength or energy from the spiritual hearth. You may choose to designate it in a different way, such as hanging a particular piece of artwork there or positioning a small wall shelf with an oil lamp on it, or any other method you feel appropriate to you and your home. You may simply use it as the place where you begin your cleaning or tidying activities. (For more information on altars and shrines, see Chapter 6.)

Ritual for Recognizing the Sanctity of the Hearth

As previously mentioned there is no need to consecrate the hearth because it is innately sacred. However, many people like to perform some kind of ritual formally recognizing an existing sanctity, and so this ritual has been included. It can be used on a regular basis as you wish or performed when you feel your focal hearth area has become cluttered with other energies that may not be negative but may occlude your personal connection to the hearth. As the hearth is your source of power and energy, keeping the connection to it clear also means that the energy flowing from it moves more freely.

The items you will need are representations of the four elements. You don't need a lot of each item; a teaspoon is enough. You may place the items in bowls before you on the floor or on a table nearby. They should be within arm's reach so that you do not need to move. The candle may be any candle at all—an emergency candle, a tea light, a birthday candle stuck into a small ball of dough or even a crumpled-up bit of tinfoil. Choose a color that resonates with the concept of hearth and home to you. The mixed herbs and spices can be drawn from your spice rack, a pinch of at least two different ones and as many as you like.

Although the directions indicate standing, you may kneel before the hearth if you are more comfortable doing the ritual that way.

You will need:

- Small bowl of salt
- Small bowl of water

- Small bowl of mixed herbs and spices from your kitchen
- Matches
- Candle in candleholder (color of your choice)
- Heatproof dish
- Small bowl of olive or vegetable oil

1. Stand before your hearth. Close your eyes and take three deep, cleansing breaths, inhaling and exhaling slowly, with the intent of calming your body and mind. Be in the moment.

2. Open your eyes and hold your hands out to the hearth. Say:

    Heart of my home,
    I recognize you.
    My spirit feels your warmth.
    My soul feels your wisdom.
    Sacred hearth, I recognize you.

3. Bow to the hearth.

4. Press your fingers into the bowl of salt, then say, *Sacred hearth, the earth of my home recognizes your sanctity.* Flick your fingers so that the grains of salt clinging to them scatter toward and over the hearth area.

5. Dip your fingers into the water, then say, *Sacred hearth, the water of my home recognizes your sanctity.* Flick your fingers so that the droplets of water on them scatter over the hearth area.

6. Dip your fingers into the bowl of spices and stir them so that the scent is released, then say, *Sacred hearth, the air of my home recognizes your sanctity.* Waft your hand over the bowl, moving the scented air toward the hearth.

7. Strike a match and light the candle. Extinguish the match, laying it in a heatproof dish. Pick up the candle and hold it toward the hearth, saying, *Sacred hearth, the fire of my home recognizes your sanctity.*

8. Place the candle on the hearth itself, saying, *Sacred hearth, I honor the sacred fire that burns within you. I thank you for the wisdom, knowledge, and power that you bring to this home. May your sacred flame burn forever, and may my home be ever blessed by it.*

9. Dip a finger into the oil, saying, *Sacred hearth, with this oil I mark you as a symbol of our recognition of your sanctity and our gratitude for your many gifts and blessings.* Touch your oil-damp fingertip to the hearth. As your hearth may indeed be a symbolic space, make sure to not smear too much oil; a light touch will suffice.

10. Bow to the hearth one last time. Leave the candle burning if you will be working in the room; otherwise, snuff it out.

Your Imagined Spiritual Hearth

One of the things you can do to further develop your perception of your spiritual hearth is to create one in your imagination. This imagined version in no way replaces or supersedes the location of the spiritual hearth in your home. Instead, think of it as your idealized version of the spiritual hearth, a place you can visit in your mind while meditating or allowing your thoughts to wander. An imagined landscape such as this offers you unlimited access to another representation of your spiritual hearth, one that you can carry with you wherever you go. It's also a place where you can carry out activities in which you can't necessarily engage in the everyday world for whatever reason (lack of space, lack of privacy, limited physical capability, and so forth). Think of it as your virtual spiritual hearth, linked to both the physical representation of your spiritual hearth and the actual spiritual heart of your home. Your imagined spiritual hearth can be a mental reflection of the actual physical place you have set up, or it can be an idealized spiritual hearth.

To create your imagined hearth:

1. Sit in the spiritual heart of your home, in front of the physical representation you have created or chosen.

2. Light a candle or oil lamp to represent the sacred flame of light and love that burns in the heart of the spiritual hearth.

3. Relax your body and close your eyes, breathing deeply and slowly. Visualize a flame, such as the one you have lit. Now slowly expand your visualization to see what kind of surface the flame is resting on. What is the light like? What is the room or area around the flame like? Look at the walls (if there are any), the ground, the ceiling, or the sky. These things tend to appear in this way for a reason, usually created by your subconscious mind. You may change these things as you desire, but think about why they have appeared in your imagination in these forms.

You are free to design your virtual spiritual hearth as you wish, but keep it simple. Remember that you are creating a space in which you want to feel safe, relaxed, serene, and still connected to your home. The space you visualize may not be very different from the physical representation you have created for your spiritual hearth, and that's absolutely fine.

When you are finished, take some time to write down or draw what your imagined spiritual hearth looks like. Include these notes and sketches in your kitchen journal (see Chapter 8). If you like, you can perform a version of the previous ritual to recognize the sanctity of the hearth in your imagination too. Simply visualize performing the ritual in your virtual spiritual hearth.

Accessing the Energy of Your Spiritual Hearth

One of the reasons for creating and maintaining a spiritual hearth is the power and energy that it provides for the household. It's a symbiotic relationship: the household creates energy that feeds the spiritual hearth, which in turn nourishes and lends power to the household.

Theoretically you are always connected to your spiritual hearth, but at times it can be hard to sense the connection, especially when you are tired or stressed. When you are in need of energy to replenish your own or to shore you up, you have two options: you can draw on your spiritual hearth, or you can draw on the energy of the earth. The latter is a technique called grounding.

To draw on the energy of the earth, imagine your personal energy extending a tendril of awareness down through the water, through the earth under the building, to the center of the earth. Feel how rooted you are, how connected to the world and its energy.

You can also use this technique to access the energy of your spiritual hearth. Visualize a tendril of your awareness extending to your spiritual hearth, wherever you feel that may be. You might visualize the physical location within your home that you have designated your spiritual hearth or a shrine you have constructed (see Chapter 6), or you might reach out for the feeling the energy of your spiritual hearth creates. Through that tendril, absorb the energy of your spiritual hearth. Withdraw the tendril back into your energy center when you are done.

If you're unfamiliar with grounding or would like a more structured technique, here's a more detailed step-by-step process for drawing on the energy of your spiritual hearth.

1. Visualize your physical representation of your spiritual hearth or your virtual hearth. Imagine yourself standing before it.
2. Visualize a flame burning on it—a candle, an oil lamp, a needfire, or some other form. This flame represents the spiritual power of your hearth, the energy you and your family have put into it as well as the energy it produces on its own.
3. Hold your hands out to it. Imagine your hands feeling the warmth of the flame. The warmth is a form of that spiritual energy.

4. Draw that warmth into your hands and feel it flow up your arms and into your body. Let it fill up your heart and spirit. Absorb as much as you need.

5. When you feel energized, balanced, relaxed, or however you wanted the spiritual hearth to make you feel, move your hands away from the flame and place your palms together. This closes the energy connection you have made to the flame and prevents you from absorbing too much of the energy.

6. Thank your spiritual hearth in your own words and allow the visualization to fade. Open your eyes and take a few deep, slow breaths. Make sure you feel yourself fully back in the moment. Stretch gently if you like.

If you prefer an alternate visualization, instead of feeling the warmth of the flame, visualize yourself absorbing the light the flame casts and absorb the energy that way.

You can also channel this energy into objects or spaces as necessary. Visualize one hand absorbing the energy of the spiritual hearth and extend your other hand toward the object or area you wish to fill or empower with the energy of the spiritual hearth. This goal or target may be physically located in the real world with you or elsewhere, or it may be something intangible, such as a situation. With this method, you are acting as a conduit: the hearth's energy passes through you and into the target.

Cauldron and Water Energy at the Spiritual Hearth

Usually the energy of the spiritual hearth is referred to in terms of light and heat. This is a direct result of the primary connection between the hearth and sacred fire. However, if working with fire energy is uncomfortable for you, simply replace the visualization of a flame with a cauldron of cool water imbued with healing, comfort, and serenity. For example, in the previous visualization, you can imagine placing your hands in the cauldron of water to draw the coolness of the energy up, or simply cup your hands around the cool cauldron and absorb the energy that way. (The cauldron as a symbol is explored in Chapter 4.) Experiment with both the fire and cauldron visualizations, get to know how your personal energy reacts with each symbol and kind of energy, and use them in different situations.

Incorporating Your Ancestors

Family is one of your connections to life. They are a source of strength as well as something to protect and care for. Living or dead, they contribute to the energy of your home. Acknowledging the contribution of ancestors, be they biological or spiritual, is a way of honoring their contribution to the world in which you live and also of maintaining continuity of tradition. Expressing your gratitude and respect for them is one way to touch that sacred space symbolized by the hearth.

There's a lot of emotional energy tied up with home-based activity, especially in creating favorite family foods. Challenge someone on how they prepare a dish considered a family specialty, and you're liable to encounter aggressive defense, if not an all-out attack. They may defend their methods and by extension those family members from whom they learned them. "My mother always did it this way" is something you may often say in the kitchen, whether you're making gravy, rolling gnocchi, adding a pinch of a certain secret ingredient to a soup or stew, sweeping the floor after scattering salt on it, or soaking linen napkins after use. You absorb a lot of tradition in and around the kitchen simply by being exposed to how someone else performs tasks, and by replicating those techniques you are in essence maintaining a tradition of sorts.

Many cultures honor or worship their ancestors. "When you drink water, think of its source" is a Chinese saying that illustrates the impact and presence ancestors can have upon your life and spiritual practice. The saying suggests that through acknowledging your ancestors you are not alone, that you come from somewhere; your ancestors anchor you in the world. Essentially, you owe what you are and what you have to work with to those who came before you.

Ancestors are always a part of the spiritual hearth's energy. Ancestors are tied into the concept of hearth and home, both as family and as guiding energies. Like the hearth itself, your ancestors are a source of inspiration, energy, and support, a place of safety and restoration for you and your current family.

There is no hard-and-fast rule dictating how to incorporate ancestors into your spiritual practice. Simply remembering them ties their energy into your home and your life. Actively honoring them with words or actions further weaves their energy into the wellspring of energy that is maintained by your spiritual hearth. It may be enough for you to know and understand that they have had an effect upon you and who you are today. If you wish to honor them in a more structured fashion, try making an ancestor shrine. It doesn't have to be complicated; it can be as simple as placing a photograph of a relative who meant a lot to you near the spiritual heart of your home, or an item that belonged to them, or a small assembly of objects that you associate with your ancestors. Ancestors are not limited to biological relatives, either. Spiritual ancestors are people who have somehow shaped your outlook or way of life and whom you wish to honor or remember in some way. When calling upon the energy of your spiritual hearth you can wordlessly appeal to the ancestors as well or speak aloud to them and ask for their support and blessing.

Here's a sample prayer to the ancestors for guidance or thanks:

Ancestors, thank you for being here with me and my family.
Guide us daily, and help us to make the right choices.
Be our strength and our comfort,

And help protect this home.
Thank you for your lives and your accomplishments.
Ancestors, we thank you.

At this point you may make an offering to them. Offerings are a sign of respect, not necessarily a sign of worship, and can be anything suitable. Ancestor honoring in many neo-pagan paths involves offering a small portion of something a specific ancestor enjoyed in life, but if you are calling upon your ancestors in general, then something like a small thimbleful of tea, wine, or the food you are preparing is ideal.

If you don't know very much about your ancestors, try asking living relatives about their parents or grandparents. They may know stories that reveal hints about the ancestor's personality or activities. Genealogical research is another avenue you may wish to follow if the idea of ancestor energy particularly interests you. Learn as much as you can about ancestors, both biological and spiritual. Let them be a source of inspiration for you.

Chapter 4

The Magic of the Cauldron

THE CAULDRON IS A SYMBOL found in many cultures and folktales. Closely associated with the hearth, the cauldron, along with the sacred fire, functions as a central symbol in the practice of hearthcraft and is a focal image in the house witch's spirituality.

What Is a Cauldron?

The origin of the word *cauldron* comes from the Latin *caldarium*, meaning "hot bath," or from *caldaria*, "cooking pot." And the cauldron is essentially a large metal pot used for cooking over an open fire. The cauldron was (and still is, in many countries) an essential vessel in hearthside cooking. It has thus been commonly used throughout the ages until relatively recently.

It was often set on a tripod rack or made with feet in order to set it in the embers or next to them, depending on what needed to be cooked. A curved handle was often also used to suspend it from a hook in the fireplace over the fire.

Like wells, cauldrons are connections to the Otherworld, a place of mysticism, the dead, enlightenment, and a realm of the Divine, whence come inspiration and Divine healing. The cauldron may also be seen as a symbol of initiation, wherein a symbolic death and rebirth are experienced. The cauldron is generally considered a feminine symbol, like most cups or bowl-shaped dishes. It is also associated with the element of water.

At its most basic, the cauldron is associated with the everyday magic of cookery, the combination of ingredients and application of heat to create something new, which is nourishing, therapeutic, or supportive in some way. As a result of its practical physical use, the cauldron has become a symbol of abundance, source, warmth, nourishment, and transformation.

Transformation and transmutation are two of the most common themes associated with the cauldron in myth and story. To transform is to undergo or initiate change in form or appearance. To transmute, however, is to change in substance and is a term often used in chemistry or alchemy to describe the changing of one element into another. A cauldron not only visibly alters something on the outside (transform); it also alters it on a very basic level, changing its very nature (transmute).

Symbolically, the cauldron offers you the opportunity to explore your inner self, the deep, dark well of your emotional nature. It can symbolize the repository of inner wisdom and hidden knowledge. Like the associations with the element of water in Western occult tradition, it can stand for the subconscious realm, the source of dreams, intuition, and healing.

The cauldron is sometimes associated with the Underworld, particularly in classical Greek and Roman iconology and belief (the cauldron suggests the shape of a cave, which was a place often sacred to chthonic goddesses), as well as the Otherworld, which is often reached through a body of water, according to several cultural mythos.

Cauldrons in Mythology

Cauldrons have figured largely in mythology, especially Celtic mythology. As you read over the following myths, notice how the cauldron can be seen as a contained, controlled place for transformation. As a ritual vessel, the cauldron serves as a focus for transformative energies. It can represent the source or the destination. It can symbolize wisdom, change, descent into the unknown, or rebirth. It's a wonderfully adaptive symbol.

It is very interesting to note that the cauldron dispenses both wisdom and nourishment in these mythological tales. The parallel between the two suggests that wisdom nourishes the spirit, while food nourishes the body; a balance is created between the two. Equally, the spirit must be nourished by inspiration and wisdom, just as the body is nourished by food.

The traits of the separate mythological cauldrons tend to be synthesized by virtue of their similar root symbol, and thus one can encounter references to cauldrons that heal and feed and offer knowledge, all in one. Here are some of the most famous cauldrons and their stories.

The Cauldron of Cerridwen

Cerridwen is the Welsh goddess of grain and prophecy, generally perceived as a dark crone goddess. The cauldron she guards is the cauldron of Otherworld inspiration and Divine knowledge. The most famous appearance of this cauldron is in the story of the birth of Taliesin, one of the most famous poets of the Celtic nation. Cerridwen set the boy Gwion Bach to stirring a potion she was brewing in her cauldron for a year and a day, intending the potion to bestow knowledge of all things past, present, and future upon her own son. On the final day three hot drops splashed from the cauldron onto Gwion Bach's thumb, and he instinctively lifted it to his mouth to cool it. With this act the potion's power transferred to him, rendering the rest of the brew useless. With the acquisition of such knowledge, Gwion Bach knew that Cerridwen would pursue him to punish him, and he fled, changing shape into first a hare, then a fish, then a grain of wheat to hide from her. Cerridwen did pursue him, changing shape to better hunt him as first a greyhound, then an otter, then a hen, swallowing the grain of wheat in triumph. Instead of consuming Gwion, however, Cerridwen found that she was pregnant, and gave birth to Gwion again. She sewed him in a leather bag and threw him into the sea, where he was found by a fisherman who named him Taliesin for his white brow.

The Cauldron of the Dagda

The Dagda is a father and fertility god of the Irish Tuatha Dé Danaan. His cauldron was known as Undry (or the Coire Anseasc) and possessed the power of producing plentiful, abundant food, capable of feeding an army without exhausting itself. A pertinent phrase often associated with the Dagda's cauldron is "No one ever went away from it hungry," an important concept when taken in the context of hearth and hospitality. In some versions of the Dagda's mythology, the cauldron produces food only in proportion with a man's merit. Some sources also attach the power of healing to the cauldron of the Dagda.

Also key to the precepts of hospitality, the Dagda's cauldron is said to be the resting place of the fiery-hot Spear of Lugh, one of the four treasures of Tuatha Dé Danaan. This pairing demonstrates the peaceful and calming nature of the cauldron containing the dangerous and warlike spear.

The Cauldron of Medea

Greek mythology tells us that Medea was a sorceress. When Jason came to Colchis on his quest to acquire the

Golden Fleece, Medea, the daughter of King Aeëtes of Colchis, who kept the fleece, fell in love with him and promised to help him in return for his promise to marry her and take her with him when he left. Jason agreed, and with Medea's help he passed each of the challenges. After other encounters they arrived in Iolicus, ruled by Jason's usurping uncle Pelias. Medea brought about his death by telling his daughters that she could revive and rejuvenate people by dismembering them and plunging them into her cauldron. She demonstrated this by dismembering an old goat or sheep and throwing the pieces into the cauldron, which was filled with herbs and a magical brew. A young living kid or lamb leapt out of the cauldron. The daughters agreed to do the same for their father, but Medea prepared the cauldron differently, filling it with water and only a few simple herbs. When the daughters dismembered Pelias and threw the pieces into the cauldron, without the brew of herbs and other preparations Medea had made, their plan failed and Pelias was dead.

Medea also used her cauldron at Jason's request to rejuvenate his father Aeson. Among other ritual activities, she combined herbs, flowers, seeds, stones, sand, frost, and parts of animals known for their vigor and long life. When the olive branch with which she was stirring the potion sprouted leaves and fruit, Medea knew the brew was ready. She cut the throat of the old man and let all his blood run out, then poured the brew into his mouth and the wound on his throat. He grew forty years younger.

Medea was the granddaughter of Helios, the god of the sun, as well as the niece of the sorceress Circe. Perhaps most importantly, she was a priestess of Hecate, a goddess of the Underworld, and it was primarily from her that she drew her power. The cauldron is a critical element of Medea's rejuvenation magic, which suggests that it belongs to the tradition of cauldrons that restore life.

The Cauldron of Bran

From the annals of Welsh mythology comes the cauldron of Bran the Blessed, known as the Cauldron of Rebirth. Bran the Blessed gave it as a conciliatory gift to his new brother-in-law Matholwch, the king of Ireland, who married Bran's sister Branwen and whose horses were mutilated in anger by Bran's half-brother Efnisien. The cauldron was considered part of Branwen's dowry and was taken back to Ireland when the two returned.

Bran's cauldron has the ability to resurrect the dead. Immersing a man in the cauldron renders him alive and in peak physical condition by the next day, but those who are resurrected cannot talk. This is because they have been to the land of the dead and may not speak of what they saw there to the living. Unfortunately for Bran, the cauldron was used against him and his men when they later found themselves at war with the Irish: the king of Ireland repeatedly resurrected his slain warriors and returned them to battle. Bran's half-brother eventually broke the cauldron, sacrificing himself to do so.

The cauldron was said to have origins in Ireland under a lake. This further reinforces the rebirthing tradition, for the cauldron, like the lake, is a point of connection or interaction between the world of humans and the Otherworld.

The Cauldron of Annwn

The quest for the cauldron of Annwn is chronicled in the Welsh poem "Preiddeu Annwn" ("The Spoils of Annwn"), from the Book of Taliesin, which dates from somewhere between the ninth and twelfth centuries. Annwn is the Welsh Otherworld. One of the functions of the Celtic Otherworld is as a land of the dead. King Arthur and his companions travel to Caer Sidi, a fortress on an island ruled by the Lord of Annwn, and therefore they are essentially traveling to the land of the dead on this quest to obtain the cauldron belonging to the Lord of Death. The cauldron is enameled with flowers and studded with pearls or diamonds, cooled by the pure breath of nine maidens who protect it. One of the magical properties of this cauldron is that it will not boil the food of a coward or one who is forsworn. It is so well protected that only Arthur and six other men return from this quest. They secure the cauldron, but at great cost.

A cauldron belonging to the Lord of Death can be assumed to be a cauldron like that of Bran the Blessed, one that rejuvenates or restores life.

The Cauldron of Brigid

The Irish goddess Brigid (paralleled by Brid in Scotland and Brigantia in Britain, among others) is sometimes said to possess or carry a cauldron. This is a logical development from the extant Brigid myths, for Brigid is not only a goddess of inspiration; she is also a goddess of healing, associated with wells and water, and a goddess of fire and smithcraft. The cauldron is a water symbol and is closely associated with fire for its connection to hearth and home, and also smithcraft, the method by which cauldrons are made.

Brigid is a goddess of three aspects, meaning there are three separate goddesses each called Brigid governing the realms of healing, poetry, and smithcraft. The smith aspect is known as Begoibne, which means "woman of the smithy." Begoibne was said to have a smithy under Croghan Hill in Ireland, where, among other things, she forged cauldrons wherein the future was stored.

Odrerir, the Norse Cauldron of Inspiration

In Norse mythology, Odhinn drank magical blood from a cauldron to obtain wisdom. He transformed himself into a serpent to drink all the poets' mead in the cauldron Odrerir. Odrerir is sometimes interpreted as the cauldron itself, as well as the mead of poetry inside it. The *Prose Edda* describes the blood of the god Kvasir, who was originally created from the saliva of all the gods, being blended with honey in the cauldron Odrerir by dwarfs. The resulting liquid was the mead drunk to transform the man drinking it into a skald, or scholar-poet. After bargaining for it by exchange of work and being denied his fair payment, Odhinn tricked the keepers of this cauldron using guile and disguise, and with three swallows he drained the cauldron of the magical brew. In this way he became the god who dispenses inspiration to poets, in a sense liberating the cauldron from the giant Suttungr, who jealously guarded it. This mead was also used by the Valkyries to restore life to the slain warriors who were taken to Valhalla.

Using the Cauldron in Hearthcraft

If there is one tool that anyone following a hearth- and home-based spiritual path should have, it would be the cauldron. For all its symbolism and practical association with the hearth throughout history, the cauldron embodies so many of the goals and areas considered important in hearthcraft: abundance, nourishment, spiritual rejuvenation, introspection, and wisdom, to name only a few.

As hearthcraft is also about practicality, the cauldron isn't simply a symbol; it can be used in everyday activity as well, if you so desire. The modern kitchen cauldron is known as a Dutch oven, available with and without legs depending on indoor or outdoor use, and made of cast iron or enamelware.

If you acquire a cauldron solely for ritual or spiritual use, it doesn't have to be cast iron. While hearthcraft tends to be very practical and doesn't specify having a set of tools exclusively for ritual use, you may want to have two cauldrons: one heavy cast-iron Dutch oven–type for cooking, and a smaller, lighter one for spiritual work and as a symbol on a shrine or altar. After all, lugging a twenty-five-pound Dutch oven around can be a bit taxing.

When looking for a cauldron for spiritual work, keep in mind that you're going to want something that you can clean easily, as well as something that won't break or take up too much room; you may want to keep it out, on your altar or shrine, for example, to use for offerings or to serve as a candleholder (a tea light in a small cauldron offers the image and feel of a needfire without the mess). Or you might use your cauldron as a focus for small honoring rituals or as a visual focus during meditation.

In Chapter 6 you'll learn how to create a kitchen shrine. As a part of that shrine, you can use a small cauldron to hold a small amount of salt. The salt in your shrine or altar cauldron can be used for many things:

• The salt can absorb negative energy in the space. If placed on the shrine with this intention, the salt will absorb negative energy, but don't use that salt for cooking, as representative of earth in a ritual, or for purifying anything.

• Offer a pinch of this salt at the beginning or end of every day to the spirits of your hearth.

• Add a pinch of this salt to your cooking and visualize it banishing anything negative that lingers or as the catalyst that combines and binds the desired energies already present.

Having a small symbolic cauldron is a practical way to incorporate the energies associated with it into your home without having to store a huge cast-iron pot somewhere. Small iron cauldrons, small enough to hold in the palm of your hand up to the size of two fists together, are easily placed somewhere about your workspace without cluttering it up.

Uses for Your Cauldron

Be imaginative! The cauldron can be used in several different ways. Here are some suggestions to get you thinking about how you can involve the symbol of the cauldron into your spiritual practice and your daily work in and around the hearth:

- Use your cauldron as a candleholder by slipping a tea light into it or by filling it half full of sand or non-clumping kitty litter and placing a votive on top. Push the votive slightly into the sand so that it is steady before lighting it.
- Put a layer of sand or non-clumping kitty litter in the bottom of your cauldron and place incense sticks in it, inserting the base of the stick firmly into the sand. Mound the sand around it if you have to in order to keep it upright. (If your incense is the wooden-stick type, you can also snap some of the bare stick off.)
- Place a bit of food in your cauldron as an offering and place it on your shrine or altar.
- Put a pinch of whatever herbs or spices you are using to season your food in the cauldron on the shrine or altar.
- Place your cauldron in the center of your kitchen and visualize all the stagnant and negative energy spiraling

into it from wherever it may be hiding—corners, behind the fridge, under the stove, under the sink, and so on.

• When you need to calm yourself, set the cauldron on the table in front of you and breathe deeply to settle yourself. Visualize the darkness at the bottom of the cauldron being a portal to deep, soothing, cool energy. As you inhale, sense that energy flowing up to you. Feel the soothing energy fill you, relaxing tension, calming anger or fears. Do this until you feel calm again.

• When you need to energize yourself, set the cauldron on the table in front of you and breathe deeply to settle yourself. Visualize the darkness at the bottom of the cauldron being a portal to a vibrant, joyful energy. As you inhale, sense that energy flowing up to you. Feel the energizing energy fill you, wakening your cells and energizing your body and mind. Do this until you feel ready to take on whatever task you have been preparing for.

• Bring in flowers from your garden or that you have collected on a walk through your neighborhood. Place them in the cauldron on your altar or shrine. Remove them at the end of the day.

The Cauldron As a Meditative Focus

Use your cauldron as a meditative focus while saying a prayer or invocation. You can either gaze at the cauldron alone or fill it with water and gaze into it. Here are some ideas for prayers to say before you meditate or to wrap up a meditation session. These are only suggestions; feel free to write and use your own.

Cauldron Prayer for Abundance

As a symbol of abundance, the cauldron really can't be beaten. Abundance encompasses things like prosperity, plenty of food, good friends, a healthy bank account, and so forth.

> *Blessed cauldron,*
> *I invoke through thee Undry,*
> *The great cauldron of the Dagda.*
> *Be for me a source of abundance,*
> *Nourishing energy, and strength.*

Cauldron Prayer for Inspiration

No matter what our métier—cooking, painting, writing, singing, parenting, answering phones, or driving a bus—there are days when we feel that everything we do is bland or unoriginal. If you feel like you need a bit of supportive inspiration from your spiritual hearth, try calling on Odhinn's cauldron of poets' mead for a creative pick-me-up.

> *Blessed cauldron,*
> *I invoke through thee the cauldron of Odhinn.*
> *Be for me a source of inspiration,*
> *That my work at hearth and in home be motivated by*
> *Divine insight, handled with sensitive perception,*
> *And carried out with poetry.*

Cauldron Prayer for Spiritual Renewal

We all need to reinvent ourselves once in a while, especially if our lives feel stagnant or if we feel like we're getting nowhere. This prayer calls for figurative rebirth to help you get moving again. Remember: to be reborn, you need to give up what you currently have, so this prayer can initiate some changes in your life with which you may not be completely comfortable. It can be hard to give up ingrained ways of thinking, even if you know they're holding you back.

Blessed cauldron,
I invoke through thee the cauldron of Bran.
Wash me clean of what I no longer need,
And grant me new sight, new understanding,
And new energy to live my life.

Cauldron Prayer for Wisdom

Wisdom differs from knowledge in that it is the accumulation of enlightenment derived from putting knowledge into use, thereby gaining personal experience. Wisdom is what guides us in making decisions related to moral or ethical issues.

Blessed cauldron,
I invoke through thee the cauldron of Cerridwen.
Be for me a source of wisdom,
That I may keep peace and equilibrium within my house,
And that all who step to my hearth know right from wrong.
Grant me insight, blessed cauldron,
And aid me in my daily decisions.

Types of Cauldrons

Early cauldron-like containers were made of dried and hollowed gourds or earthen clay, but as humankind learned how to mine and work metal, it was customary to form cooking vessels of that material, as such vessels are placed in or near fire in order to heat and cook the contents. In this way, a metal cauldron may be seen as being associated with the symbol of fire, as fire is used to forge earth's metals; a symbol of water, as the element of water is used to cool it; and a symbol of earth, as the metals were extracted from the earth.

Even more correctly, however, the cauldron may be said to symbolize the interaction of these three elements and thus is a symbol of transformation. The association of transformation is also derived from the alchemy of cooking that takes place inside the vessel.

The metals commonly used to make cauldrons all have their own energies, which contribute to the overall energy within your kitchen. Being aware of what your kitchen tools are made of and the associations of their constituent elements can lend your spiritual work focus and awareness. This is a brief list of the common metals used for cauldrons and the associated energies; Chapter 8 looks at the energies of the metals commonly used for cauldrons and other kitchen tools in more depth.

- **Brass:** often used as a substitute for gold, therefore: prosperity, health, fire and sun energies, protection, attraction magic, deflecting of negativity.

- **Iron and Steel:** grounding, protection, deflecting magic and psychic energy, increasing physical strength.
- **Copper:** revitalizing, refreshing, healing, kindness, fertility, love, beauty, harmony, friendship, peace, balancing outgoing and incoming energies, attracting money.
- **Aluminum:** travel, communication, mental activity, flexibility.
- **Tin and Pewter:** money, business success, fame and renown, legal issues.

Caring for a Cast-Iron Cauldron

It's important to know how to take care of a cauldron if you wish to have it around for a while. Before you use the cauldron as anything more than a visual symbol, it must be prepared and sealed, a process known as seasoning. New cast ironware is often a dull silvery color, but cast iron that has been used is black. This does not affect the efficiency. Raw cast iron is very porous, and it has to be sealed before you use it. This is called seasoning the pot.

Make sure to wash your new cast-iron pot well with soap and hot water before seasoning it to remove any coating the production company may have put on it. If you've bought a secondhand cast-iron cauldron at a flea market or garage sale and it's rusty, it can very easily be salvaged: scrub it down with a steel-wool pad, then wash it well in hot, soapy water and season it as directed here.

1. Preheat the oven to 250–300°F.
2. Rub the cauldron inside and out with shortening or lard. (Vegetable or olive oil usually leaves a somewhat sticky residue, so avoid them.)
3. Set the cauldron on a foil-lined baking sheet and place the sheet in the preheated oven. After 15 minutes, remove the cauldron with potholders and pour or wipe out any excess grease (it will have melted and collected in the cauldron).
4. Replace in the oven and bake for 1 hour. Turn off the oven and allow the cauldron to cool inside.

To care for cast-iron cookware, clean it while it is still warm by rinsing with very hot water and wiping it out with a paper towel. Make sure it is absolutely dry before you put it away. Some people say that you should never use dish soap, but the occasional wash with soap helps break down the food grease that may be left behind, which can go rancid. Never use a scrub pad, as it breaks down the seasoned surface. If you must, scrub the whole pot and then season it again as directed previously. Never allow the pot to sit with residue in it or to stay wet after you rinse it, or it will rust.

An alternative to washing the cauldron in water is cleaning it with salt.

1. Pour a 1–3 mm (just under ¼") layer of salt in the cast-iron pot or pan.
2. Heat it on the stovetop or in the oven at a very low temperature for at least a half hour. The salt will darken from the grease and dirt it absorbs.

3. Remove from heat and allow the pan and salt to cool.

4. Use a dry, stiff brush (a brush designed for cleaning woks is good; under no circumstances use steel wool!) to scrub the salt off (remember, don't rinse it with water).

5. Finish by wiping the surface down with a paper towel or a soft cloth.

The dry salt method ensures that you don't need to worry about making sure the cast iron is bone-dry before you store it, and there is no chance of rust.

To store cast-iron cookware, line the inside of the pot with a sheet of paper towel to absorb any moisture and to reduce the chance of rust. If you have a lid for your cauldron, store it off the pot itself so as to allow the air to circulate freely around it; this also reduces the chance of rusting.

Blessing Your Cauldron

When you acquire a cauldron, it's best to cleanse and purify it before use for either cooking or as a spiritual symbol or tool. You can adapt the Basic Room Purification Ritual in Chapter 7 or create your own. Once the vessel has been purified, you may say a blessing over it, such as this one or another of your choosing, or you may write one of your own.

Cauldron,
Sacred symbol of rebirth,
Of transformation and wisdom,

Share with me your secrets and insight.
May my life be touched by your energy
As we work together.
Cauldron, I welcome you into my home.
Blessings upon you.

If you like, you can sprinkle a few fresh or dried herbs inside the pot that represent blessing or welcome to you. (If you don't have any connection to herbs or sense an energy like this in any of them, check the appendix for a brief list of suggested herbs and their traditional associations.)

Recipe: Cauldron Cookies

These fun little treats are a version of thumbprint cookies. Use the well in the center as the source for whatever you empower: nuts for abundance and fertility, and so forth. Cauldron cookies can be made and empowered with whatever energy you wish to associate with them, such as wisdom, abundance, or spiritual transformation. (See Chapter 9 for more information on the spiritual aspect of cooking and using food in a spiritual context.)

This recipe uses cocoa to make a chocolate cookie, which looks more like the traditional dark cauldron. If you wish to make a vanilla cookie, leave out the cocoa and add an extra spoonful or two of flour.

Make sure you press your thumb into these cookies very deeply. If you only make a light impression the cauldron-like well is lost when the cookie bakes and rises slightly. Alternatively, you may bake them for 4 or 5 minutes, then press your thumb into the cookies (carefully as they will be hot) and bake them for the remaining time.

You will need:

- 1 cup butter, softened
- 1 cup brown sugar
- 2 large eggs
- ¼ cup milk
- 1 teaspoon vanilla extract
- 2 cups flour
- ⅔ cup cocoa
- 1 teaspoon baking powder
- ½ teaspoon salt
- Filling suggestions: jam, whipped cream, lightly crushed berries sprinkled with a bit of sugar (let this mixture sit at least 1 hour before filling the cookies), frosting, nut butter

1. In a large mixing bowl, cream the butter. Add the sugar and beat until fluffy. Add eggs one at a time and blend in. Add milk and vanilla and blend carefully. Mix well.
2. In a medium bowl, whisk together flour, cocoa, baking powder, and salt. Fold into the butter mixture carefully, then mix until well blended.
3. Cover bowl with plastic wrap and refrigerate for at least 1 hour or until firm enough to handle.
4. Heat oven to 350°F. Roll dough into 1" balls. Place on lightly greased baking sheets. Press thumb deeply but gently in center of each ball. (Dusting your hands with icing sugar may

help prevent the dough from sticking too much while rolling the balls and pressing your thumb into them.)

5. Bake 10–12 minutes or until set. Cool slightly on baking sheet, then remove from sheet to finish cooling on a wire rack. Cool completely before filling. If you want to carry the cauldron theme further, use thin strips of licorice candy as handles.

Your physical representation of the spiritual hearth or your kitchen altar or shrine is the perfect place for your ritual cauldron to rest. As the cauldron is one of the focal symbols of hearthcraft, having it within sight while you work is ideal. Glancing at it now and again can help you refocus on whatever your spiritual purpose is: nourishing, loving, protecting, or whatever may be the theme of your work.

Chapter 5

Hearth and Home Deities

THERE ARE A MULTITUDE OF DEITIES and spirits associated with the hearth, demonstrating the spiritual importance of this area. The concepts of hearth and home are so completely intertwined that deities associated with one are generally associated with the other. Here, then, is a sample of various hearth and domestic deities from several different cultures. It is by no means exhaustive, nor are the entries complete.

Hestia

The Greek goddess of the hearth, Hestia was the deity to whom offerings were made before any other. The saying "Hestia comes first" points to how entrenched she was in the lives and spiritual practice of these people. The *Homeric Hymn* "To Hestia" says,

Hestia, in the high dwellings of all, both deathless gods and men who walk on earth, you have gained an everlasting abode and highest honour: glorious is your portion and your right. For without you mortals hold no banquet, where one does not duly pour sweet wine in offering to Hestia both first and last.

Despite her first-among-equals position, Hestia is rarely referred to in myth; there are very few stories involving her, and her behavior is passive when she does appear. She seems to be more of an unembodied ideal than an enfleshed deity, as the other Olympians are presented in stories. This does not mean that she did not play a significant role in the lives of the Greeks. On the contrary: because Hestia was ever-present in the form of the home hearth as well as the public hearth, she was understood to be so entrenched in daily life that stories painting her as larger than life were unnecessary.

One of the three original Greek goddesses of the first generation of Olympians, Hestia was considered a virgin goddess, not beholden or subservient to any other person or deity. As a hearth goddess she was associated with the baking of bread and the preparation of meals. Identified also with the sacred flame, she was thereby connected to offerings, and she received a portion of every offering made to other gods.

Despite not having a formal temple, Hestia was honored by a public altar in the city hall, or prytaneum, where an eternal flame was kept lit. Just as the hearth represents the spiritual heart of the private home, the public hearth dedicated to Hestia was considered the heart of the city. When a new town was founded, embers from the public hearth would be carried to kindle the fire in the public hearth of the new municipality, transporting Hestia's essence and protection to bless the new settlement. Likewise, family members establishing a new home elsewhere would bring embers from their home hearth to their new hearth.

Hestia preserves the sanctity of the private home, keeping it a refuge and a place of spiritual renewal. The hearth was considered the spiritual heart of the private home, and the fire in it was not extinguished. If it did go out, rituals of purification and renewal were necessary to relight it. As Hestia was the essence of the home, formalized worship was effectively nonexistent; everyone honored her on an individual basis. Hestia is an example of how holy the hearth and hearth fire were considered to be and how sacred the home as temple was for a family.

Her presence is symbolized by a flame burning on the hearth or altar. Hestia is rarely portrayed in iconology, for she is understood to be the flame itself. If portrayed, however, she is sometimes shown with a flowering branch, a kettle or cauldron-shaped pot, or a torch.

It is very interesting that Hestia is seen as an old maid or homebody, terms that generally have pejorative or dismissive associations in modern society. It should be remembered that older women were considered wise and experienced and were honored in ancient societies.

Vesta

The Roman cognate of Hestia is Vesta, and while performing a similar function and position, Vesta is not precisely equal to the Greek goddess of the hearth. A major difference is that Vesta's worship was formalized, and an order of priestesses served her in formal temples. Vesta's temple housed an eternal flame that symbolized the life and safety of the city of Rome itself. It was guarded and watched over by a group of priestesses dedicated to the service of Vesta called the *Vestales*, or Vestals. These priestesses swore to devote their lives to Vesta and thus pledged celibacy for thirty years in order to devote all their energy and time to serving the goddess, giving rise to the descriptive name "the Vestal virgins."

Vesta's sacred fire was relit every first of March. A sample of the fire was taken and kept safe in a container. After the hearth was cleaned, the fire was lit again from the embers kept safe from the original fire. In this sense, the eternal flame was truly eternal, the essence of the previous year's flame and all the years before it being passed on in the embers to the new fire. The remains of sacrificial fires in the temple were also considered sacred, and the ashes were collected and stored under the temple until the yearly procession to the Tiber River, where they were thrown in. Vesta's festival was known as the Vestalia and was celebrated from June 7 to June 15.

Like Hestia, Vesta's presence is symbolized by a flame burning on an altar or the hearth of the home. Iconology depicts her with a javelin and/or an oil lamp.

Brigid

The much-loved Irish goddess of the home, Brigid is known by other names, such as Brid and Brigantia, in regions that later became Scotland and Britain. Brigid has three aspects: a smith, a healer, and a poet. She is strongly associated with the element of fire and, to a lesser degree, with the element of water.

All three of her aspects have bearing on the practice of hearthcraft. The smith works with the element of fire, which is, like the cauldron described in Chapter 4, an agent of transformation and transmutation. The smith also makes tools, many of them for home and homestead use such as cauldrons, hooks, nails, hearth sets (the tools for tending and cleaning the fireplace), fire irons (the metal supports that hold logs and other fuel to be burned), and so forth. Brigid's healing aspect focuses on restoring and maintaining health, one of the areas hearthcraft also touches. And the poet's inspiration is often symbolized by a flame.

Brigid has survived into the modern age as a Catholic saint whose areas of influence are certainly related to hearth and home. She is the patron saint of livestock such as sheep and cattle; dairy products such as milk and butter, as well as workers in the dairy industry (including milkmaids and dairy maids); children; poultry farmers; midwives; poets; and blacksmiths. Her many associations with house and home make her a very popular goddess with whom to work.

Brigid was worshipped, both as a goddess and later as a saint, by a circle of nineteen priestesses or nuns who tended an eternal flame. On the twentieth day the flame was said to survive without anyone visibly tending it, leading to the belief that the goddess herself tended the flame that day.

Tsao Wang

Tsao Wang is the Chinese god of the hearth, also known as the kitchen god. An image of Tsao Wang (and sometimes his wife) is kept in the kitchen, usually above or near the stove, symbolic of the god's presence. Incense is burned in his honor regularly, or other offerings are made. Tsao Wang is said to keep watch over the family through the year, and his wife records the good things said by each family member. The week before Chinese New Year, Tsao Wang is said to leave the hearth to report to heaven on the family's doings. Because a good report is desired, it is customary to offer sticky sweets to Tsao Wang, as well as wine and money in order to make his journey comfortable. The report Tsao Wang makes will determine if the family will be assigned good or bad luck for the coming year.

China and Japan have several customs and traditions surrounding hearth and home, often revolving around honoring family, ancestors, and hearth spirits. As they can't all be included here, you could do your own research to explore how much these cultures respect the spirits associated with the sacred space of home and the various traditions ranging from feasts and specific foods to offerings and festivals.

During the period when Tsao Wang is gone, the image is turned to face the wall, or if it is paper, it is burned. Before Tsao Wang returns, the house must be cleaned thoroughly to banish any ill luck or negative energy that is present, with every member of the family or resident of the house helping to ensure good fortune in the coming year. (The house must not be cleaned in the days immediately following the New Year, or the good luck may be lost.) The image is then turned right way round again to symbolize his return, or a new image is brought in to replace the one that was burned. A special meal is then prepared to welcome him back to the hearth.

Kamui-fuchi

Kamui-fuchi is a Japanese goddess of the hearth, originally from the Ainu people. Her name means "Rising Fire Sparks Woman," and she is symbolized by the flame in the hearth. Legend has it that she never leaves a particular home, and therefore the fire is never allowed to die. She is the major overseer of the household, but as she does not leave her place there are other household spirits that report to her. She guards the home and also dispenses justice in domestic affairs.

In Ainu tradition, the hearth is also the dwelling place of the ancestors, locating them in the heart of the household. The hearth fire was also seen as a doorway through which the family could communicate with the spirit world.

Kamado-no-Kami

Kamado-no-Kami is the Japanese god of the cooking fire or stove and oven. Like Tsao Wang, Kamado-no-Kami exists in every home simultaneously. He, too, is a god of purification; however, as the fire itself is believed to be easily polluted, there are rites for purification of the fire or oven itself as well. Shrines to him are maintained in many kitchens to both help with the daily fire and restrain its dangerous nature.

Kamado is also the word for a cooking pot in some regions of Japan, and so this deity can also be associated with cauldrons. Kamado-no-Kami is one of the set of fire deities (*hi-no-kame* or *hinokame*), and his sphere of protection extends from the hearth fire to the whole household and the food prepared within it. *Kami* is the general term for "spirit," and for this to be an official part of his name signifies how central Kamado-no-Kami is to the culture. Koujin-Sama is the syncretic Shinto-Buddhist deity of the kitchen and the cooking stove. His name is an analogue of Kamado-no-Kami.

Gabija

The Lithuanian goddess of the hearth fire, Gabija (also Gabieta, Gabeta) was perceived as a protector of the household. The hearth fire was believed to be a purifying energy that would defend the house from unclean people and creatures. Tradition dictated that the hearth fire be extinguished and ritually relit every midsummer. When a fire was laid, a cup of water or beer would be left as an offering for Gabija. When the fire was banked each night, the women of the household would pray to Gabija for good fortune and safety for the family. As in the cult of Hestia, a bride would take embers from her family's hearth and use them to lay a fire in her new home. Some sources say that a pinch of salt would be tossed into the fire as an offering. Another form of this goddess, Gabjaua, was associated with grain crops and brewing.

Ertha

A domestic deity from northern Europe, Ertha is associated with earth and abundance, fate, peace, and domestic life. She is a Germanic version of Mother Earth. In some myths, she is the mother of the three Norns, triplet sisters who control fate and destiny. Divination was often a hearthside activity, and fire is often used as a divination tool, so this association makes sense. Ertha is said to have flown through the smoke of the kitchen fire to leave small presents for each member of the family at the winter solstice, a practice very similar to the activity now assigned to Santa Claus and Father Christmas.

Frigga

One of the main female deities in Norse mythology, Frigga (also known as Frigg in some sources) is a domestic goddess in the true sense of the term. Wife to Odhinn, she is considered a goddess of marriage and love, fertility, motherhood, household management, and all domestic skills. Far from being subservient, she is powerful and shares Hlidskjalf, Odhinn's high seat that looks out over the world; she is the only other god permitted to sit in this throne-like chair. She possesses the power of prophecy, although she keeps the knowledge of the future to herself. These last two facts suggest how very powerful she is and how much information she possesses about the land and areas under her rule. With this knowledge she can best arrange and perform her tasks, maintaining an environment that is calm, well-managed, and supportive for those in her care.

Frigga has companions and attendants, all associated with domestic-related virtues and paths. Eir is the goddess of healing; Hlín is a goddess of protection; Gná is a goddess of messages and communication; and Fulla is another fertility goddess.

The symbols commonly associated with Frigga are the spinning wheel and the distaff, or drop spindle. Mistletoe, a plant that possesses healing, fertility, and protective powers, is also associated with her.

Bes

The dwarf Egyptian god of protection, Bes was often depicted on household items, associating him with the general protection of the household. He is a defensive fighter god, protecting the family both inside and outside the house; he also drives away ill fortune.

Household Spirits

A household spirit is a guardian that defends the home or some specific part of it or the family members. These spirits are not formal deities or mythological figures; rather, they are unique to the hearth and family. They may be related to the ancestors, or they may be spirits of place. Household spirits are honored within the home and are often represented by small figures or paintings or engravings on household items. Household spirits are generally acknowledged by the family and are given offerings of various food and/or drinks, or are honored in other ways. In general, the cultural associations made with these spirits are of protection of the home, protection of family members, and prosperity.

The Roman cult of the hearth and family is an excellent example of how household spirits functioned within daily life and the spiritual activity of the family. The *lares familiares* of ancient Rome were spirits associated with different places or activities. The *lar familiaris* (literally a "family guardian") was a household god or spirit associated with an individual family home. A small shrine known as a *lararium* served as a home for the *lares*, appearing variously as a niche in a wall, a wall cupboard, or a freestanding cupboard. The *lararium* was placed near the hearth, the central focus of the home, or in an entryway, sometimes sharing or standing next to a shrine to Vesta. Small statues of the *lares* were placed in and around the home to protect it, sometimes on the roof or other high places. The *lar* was an essential part of family life, in both day-to-day events and formal family functions. If individuals within the family honored the *lar*, then the spirit would protect each of them and ensure they had good fortune. If an individual did not properly honor the spirit, then he or she would be ignored and denied the spirit's aid.

The *lares* had their own festival called the Compitalia, celebrated around the fourth of January. The Compitalia is associated with the concept of crossroads, an interesting symbol when you consider how much power the *lar* held to help or hinder a family. Some records suggest that there were different *lares* for different zones of the house, such as the doorways, the hearth, and so forth. The *penates*, for example, were originally spirits of the pantry and storerooms, who, when properly honored, would ensure that the family was prosperous and always had enough to eat. In Virgil's *Aeneid*, Aeneas pauses to take the small figures of the hearth gods with him as he flees. This action suggests that "home" is wherever the hearth gods are. Taking the physical representation and focus for the spirits along with him symbolizes to Aeneas transporting the entire ancestry and culture as he seeks a new home and founds a new city.

While the *lares* were literally spirits of place, remaining in the house when a family moved and protecting everyone within it regardless of station or kinship, the *manes* were the actual spirits of family ancestors and beloved dead. *Di manes* can be translated as "the good ones" or "kindly ones." These spirits protected the family itself, not the house or household servants.

Shinto, the native religion of Japan, has as one of its tenets an honor for family and tradition. A Shinto home will usually have a small shrine or altar called the *kamidama* (a "god shelf" or "spirit shelf") placed high on a wall in a central living area of the home. This altar is often a small shelf or a small house-like structure or façade, set up to house ritual objects. Traditionally, the five offerings made at a *kamidana* are rice, sake (rice wine), water, salt, and evergreen branches or incense. The tiny set of objects used on the altar for these offerings are known as *shinki* and include white ceramic vases for the evergreen branches, flasks with lids to hold blessed sake, a small dish for rice, a flask with a lid for blessed water, a small dish for salt, and a low wooden platform or tray on which to display the *shinki* set, as well as miniature replicas of the lamps found in large formal shrines. Before any offering is made, the individual must wash his or her hands well.

While the *kamidana* is not dedicated solely to the *kamadogami* or Shinto hearth gods, it is certainly one of the kinds of spirits honored there. Creating a small location such as this in which to focus your honoring of your own household spirits and ancestors is another way to explore the spirituality of the home and to honor it. (See Chapter 3 for more information about constructing a physical representation of the spiritual hearth, and Chapter 6 for more information on constructing a kitchen shrine.)

European cultures have also retained certain house spirits that have been encoded in folktales but are still referred to in modern times and remembered in cultural tradition. These spirits are generally male, often hairy, human-shaped but in smaller proportion or of miniature stature, and are generally benevolent unless provoked by disrespect or open recognition. If one of these household spirits is associated with your cultural ancestry, you may think about inviting one to take up residence in your home. Just make sure to treat it properly!

- **Brownie (Scotland, England):** A familiar household spirit, the brownie is generally described as a small brown human, dressed in tattered clothes or in nothing at all. Sometimes there are minor physical differences from humans, such as webbed hands, missing fingers, or a flat nose. Brownies are perhaps the most helpful domestic spirits one can possibly have, helping and supporting in every possible domestic activity. It is essential that a brownie receive no other sign of appreciation than a dish of rich milk or fresh bread or cake left out for him, or the brownie will leave forever. Spoken thanks and new clothes are especially forbidden. Criticism of any kind is also forbidden, for the brownie will take offense and create a complete mess while destroying household goods. Some brownies also protect their households or use playful trickery to expose household members who are lazy and skimp on their chores!

- **Boggart (England, North Country region):** Boggarts can be either helpful or malevolent spirits. They do not tend to have physical forms, although stories exist wherein specific boggarts take physical form to torment or mislead people. Boggarts are mischievous and like playing tricks, often exhibiting poltergeist-like behavior. Benevolent boggarts are brownie-like in their behavior and will help out with domestic tasks. Like a brownie, however, it must be treated well, or it can and will display destructive behavior. The Welsh *bwca* is a form of brownie.

- **Hob (England):** The hob functions much like a brownie, but instead of providing general help he focuses on one specific task. The name refers to the flat part of a range or stovetop, or the flat place or shelf by a hearth where pans could be heated or kept warm. The same cautions regarding thanking and criticizing brownies apply to hobs. The hob can be attached to a specific house or piece of land or to a family, following them if they move. The hob is also known as a hobgoblin, which is sometimes considered a nature spirit or is confused with the malicious goblin.

- *Domovoi* **(Russia):** The *domovoi* is a helpful household spirit much like the English brownie. They are described as little old men with gray beards who live under or near the hearth or sometimes the threshold of the house. While *dom* means "house," the *domovoi* is linked to the family and will move with them when properly invited. *Domovoi* sometimes help with chores, but their primary focus is on protecting the house and the residents. A portion of the evening meal is always set aside for him, and the family never refers to him by name, only by a nickname such as "old grandfather." Like most household spirits, the *domovoi* must be kept happy, or the family risks ill fortune and suffering from poltergeist-like activity.

- *Tomte* **(Sweden):** The *tomte* or *tomtar* is a house spirit, again male and ranging from a few inches to two feet tall, who is attached to a piece of land upon which a house has been built. The *tomte*'s preferred food is porridge, often with a pat of butter on top, served to him on Christmas morning. The presence of the *tomte* ensures a smoothly run and prosperous household, sometimes at the expense of neighbors who lose grain or supplies to the *tomte* as he works to keep the household under his guardianship successful. The *tomte* is gifted with incredible strength far beyond what one would imagine. In Finland this spirit is known as the *tonttu*. Images of the *tomte* as a small man with a white beard and tall pointed red hat are often seen around Christmas.

- *Nisse* (**Denmark, Norway**): A brownie-like household spirit who likes a quiet and orderly household, the *nisse* or *nis* works on household chores at night. Like the *tomte* he may stealthily acquire goods and supplies from neighbors to supplement his household's stock of goods. The *nisse*'s preferred method of being thanked is to be left a bowl of porridge with a pat of butter. His special skill is speed.

- *Kobold* (**Germany**): A *kobold* is a household spirit who can manifest as human, animal, fire, or household object. Similar to brownies and other household spirits, they are most frequently described as humans between two and four feet tall. *Kobolds* live under the hearth or in a less-trafficked area such as a woodshed or attic. They finish what chores have been left undone when the family has gone to bed, keep pests away, and help the family maintain an abundance of food and good fortune. As is customary, the *kobold* and his efforts must be respected, or the family risks losing his services and suffering dreadful misfortune, illness, and hardship. Like the Romans did with their household spirits and gods, German peasants carved effigies and small figures of *kobolds* to protect their houses. There are other kinds of *kobolds* in German mythology as well, specifically those who dwell in mines and those who work aboard ships.

Although not considered gods in a real sense, these more mischievous household spirits had to be kept content in order to avoid ill fortune or obstacles in daily life. In some cases, keeping a spirit content meant not acknowledging it, as in the case of the brownie.

Offerings to Household Spirits

Offerings are a way of honoring your chosen principles, guardians, or concepts of the sacred. The term *offering* suggests that what you are giving to the entity you are honoring is in some way precious to you. Anything can be an offering.

Every house will have different spirits, and they will all have different personalities, likes, and dislikes. Food is a simple offering that is commonly made throughout the world. In Japan, for example, the practice of scattering rice in the four corners and in the center of a particular site as an offering to a *kami* or god is called *sanku*. The basic food offerings such as sake, salt, and water are called *shinsen*, although an offering may be of any food, cooked or otherwise.

Many traditional offerings tie in to the basic foods prepared at the hearth, especially bread and porridge. A simple way to honor your house spirits is to leave a portion of the meal you are serving to your own family for them, either on your kitchen shrine or in another place. The amount depends on what you can spare or what you think the spirit would appreciate. An excessive amount might suggest to the spirit that you have more than enough and do not need help; too little may offend it. A spoonful may be enough. Leave the offering overnight and dispose of what is left the next morning. While it may not seem as if any has been consumed, the argument is often made that spirits absorb the energy of an offering, and they certainly are aware of the action and appreciate the respect and acknowledgment thus demonstrated.

Chapter 6

The Kitchen As a Sacred Space

IN TODAY'S HOMES, often the only place that approximates a hearth is the kitchen. This isn't surprising when you consider that the kitchen plays a central role in everyday life, being the place where food is prepared and eaten. House witch spirituality incorporates domestic activity of all kinds, and most domestic activity is based or originates in the kitchen, so it makes sense to establish a spiritual element there.

The Power of the Kitchen

It can be hard to shake the mindset drilled into North American culture by the technological improvements in the mid-to-late twentieth century. Advertising dating from the 1950s and 1960s repeatedly targeted wives and mothers as people who deserved to spend more time out of the kitchen to live a "real" life. Inventions and prepackaged foods to shorten time spent in the kitchen and reduce energy devoted to kitchen- and domestic-related activity have somehow led us to believe that the kitchen is a place where we ought not to be.

In a way, this is sad. It suggests that the kitchen is a place to avoid, a place where we ought to spend the least amount of time possible. We have come to regard food preparation and domestic activity as things that have to be done before we get to do the other rewarding things in life. As a friend said to me the other day, "We have to learn to understand that running a household is not only work, it's valid work. It's not something that gets squeezed in after six o'clock. It's not taking away from other things if we do it between nine and five." And she's right. The feminist revolution of the latter half of the twentieth century succeeded in opening the workplace to women, but, unfortunately, in so doing it suggested that domestic management was somehow inferior to work done elsewhere. When establishing a home-based spirituality, it's important to examine your feelings about the kitchen and the work done there. Even if you choose another room or area to be your symbolic hearth, the function of the kitchen doesn't change, and so much of domestic activity is based there that your feelings about it will certainly influence home-based spiritual work.

Kitchen History

The kitchen hasn't always been a separate room in the house. Originally it was nothing more than a cooking fire brought indoors, with the other shelter-based activity carrying on around it. As the kitchen evolved into a specialized area it became its own room, with separate areas for storage of food, equipment, and activity. The room became further separated into a hot kitchen and cold kitchen where space permitted, the hot kitchen containing the fireplace and hearth for roasting meats and making hot foods, and the cold kitchen a place of lower temperature where foods such as pastry, jellied foods, and dairy were kept or prepared.

Older kitchens were larger than the ones we use today, as they encompassed a wide variety of pursuits. Apart from cooking, activities such as eating, washing laundry, taking baths, candle-making, spinning and weaving, sewing, food preserving in all forms, nursing the sick, childcare, lessons, and countless other pursuits all took place in the kitchen of the average home.

As the twentieth century saw the invention of time- and labor-saving devices, the kitchen began to shrink in size as less time was spent there and activities were relocated to specific activity-associated areas. The trend in downsizing began to reverse in the late twentieth century. Today's kitchen designs feature layouts that have returned to an open-plan arrangement, allowing families to congregate in a larger room and share time together. There's a reason we see kitchens being designed with large work or relaxation spaces adjacent and open to the actual kitchen area and computer nooks in the kitchen itself. With less time spent in the home in general, families seek to make the most of their time together. It makes sense that families come together in the kitchen or adjacent open-plan rooms while a meal is being prepared.

The Heart of a Home

Kitchens have always changed in size and equipment according to the needs of the era. And yet throughout it all, they are continually associated with domesticity and the heart of the home. The kitchen is a key communal area in most homes: it is a meeting place; a social area; a point of communication; a place where food is stored, prepared, and consumed. All the related equipment for these activities is stored here as well.

Don't dismiss this chapter if your physical analogue or your spiritual hearth is located elsewhere in your home. The function the kitchen serves in a family's everyday life links it strongly to your hearth- and home–based spirituality.

The kitchen is the one room in the house that sees a constant stream of activity. It is seen less so nowadays, what with the use of appliances that can store and prepare food in a fraction of the time once necessary, as well as the widespread use of preprepared and prepackaged food. Historically, however, the kitchen was in constant use. It served as the headquarters of the home, a staging place for maintaining the running of the household: it was the location of the pantry and was adjacent to the storage place of foodstuffs; it was where the cooking fire resided, which required constant supervision; it was where food preparation and preservation took place; and in many cases, it was where the food was consumed as well.

In terms of hearthcraft, the kitchen as a place of physical nourishment is a logical parallel to the spiritual center of your home. If this is true for you, then setting up an altar or shrine to represent your spiritual hearth in the kitchen makes perfect sense. If your kitchen is poorly laid out or a place of stress for you, thinking about what creates an atmosphere more conducive to a spiritual environment or setting up an altar or shrine there can help you redirect, purify, or otherwise make the energy of your kitchen more appealing and make your experience there a happier and more rewarding one. If you hate your kitchen, anything that might help should be tried at least once! If in the end the kitchen is just absolutely not the heart of your home, no matter how you look at it, don't fight it; go with wherever you feel drawn to. Do your best to open yourself to the spiritual aspect of the work done in the kitchen by employing some of the techniques in this book.

Kitchen Shrines and Altars

While your entire kitchen is or can be sacred space (see the discussion on sacred space in Chapter 2), creating a defined location within the kitchen that serves as sacred space can help you focus on the spiritual aspect of hearthcraft while using the existing space in your kitchen in a practical fashion. These defined places or zones provide you with a touchstone of sorts, a place or thing that you can use to represent the greater whole.

The term *altar* can evoke the concept of something formal and untouchable. In neo-pagan usage an altar generally means simply a physical space used for magical work or worship. It provides a place of focus. A shrine is generally a specific site set up to honor an entity or principle.

Do you have to figure out which you're using in hearthcraft? No; the word isn't important. A lot of the time your altar/shrine will be a place that symbolizes or otherwise represents your connection with or to a deity, or your concept of the sacred. What you call it isn't important. In this book, both words are used to mean the same thing: the special spot in your kitchen (or elsewhere) that you have chosen to house meaningful objects and symbols, which stimulates and supports your ongoing spiritual practice.

If you intend to use it as a place to display meaningful objects connected with a hearth deity or house spirit and as a place to leave offerings, it is probably a shrine. If you intend to use it primarily as a place for some sort of eternal flame and as somewhere to put short-term spiritual items as you work with them over a short-term basis, including magical items such as sachets or empowered symbols and objects, it's probably an altar.

Altars can be designated as more active and projective, whereas shrines tend to be more passive and receptive. Does it matter if you can't define or clearly separate what you're setting up or what you intend to do at them? No. It also doesn't matter if you set one up and it slowly takes on the characteristics of the other, or if you set up one place to do double duty as both. In the end, what you're doing is creating a place to serve as a physical point of reference for your spiritual work, an interface for your communication with the Divine.

A "Home" for the Home

An altar or shrine is a created sacred space, an area set apart to honor a concept or force, a deity or spirit, or to represent your connection to the Divine. Both can represent emotions, commitments, or just about anything you desire or require. A space such as this in the hearth, the spiritual heart of the home, stands as a formal physical representation of the spiritual hearth. It provides a "home" for the symbolic hearth. A formal physical representation of the hearth makes it easier for you to visualize it and interact with it. People usually find it easier to work with a tangible representation than an abstract concept, no matter how strongly you may feel that abstract concept's presence. People like to mark the places they consider sacred in some way, partially in honor of what they feel is sacred but also to remind themselves of that sanctity and to create an analogy in the physical world.

Is it essential to have a kitchen altar or shrine? Well, yes and no. You can certainly cultivate and manage a spiritual environment without one, but it's a lot easier to do if you have a physical place where you can focus your attention now and again. A place where you can collect certain special things that symbolize or remind you of your connection to the sacred principles in your life is a unique thing. It's simply easier for most people to have a physical representation of what's going on in their heads and spirits. Human beings are somewhat magpie-like in that shiny things attract them and make them feel good. It's gratifying to have a designated place to burn candles or incense, or to leave tiny offerings to your house spirits or the universe in thanksgiving, or to put the first leaf of autumn or violet of spring.

A kitchen shrine or altar doesn't need to be something large. And that's a good thing, because space in a kitchen is generally already at a premium. Some may already consider their counters or stovetop to be sacred space, and that's fine. But one of the benefits of creating a single focal point in the kitchen to serve as a shrine is that it keeps your spiritual or magical-related work off your main everyday workspaces.

A separate altar also keeps potentially inedible materials away from places where food is prepared. And finally, it keeps things such as smoldering incense or burning candles and oil lamps safely out of harm's way. There's no rule that stipulates there can be only one such space per kitchen or home, either. If you want to set up two or more, do it! If you create a physical representation of the spiritual heart of your home, adding a kitchen shrine doesn't take away from that physical hearth.

Designing Your Shrine

There are things to consider when you design a kitchen shrine or altar. First of all, the location should be somewhere accessible, yet out of the way in order to protect the objects upon it. There's a lot of activity in the kitchen, and you don't want your shrine area to be continually disturbed; there are also the safety issues previously mentioned. Places you can consider using include:

- Above the doorframe (a narrow shelf is ideal)
- A wall shelf
- A series of narrow shelves running about a foot below the ceiling (plate rails, for example)
- On the back of the stove, along the top of the back plate (you may need to set a board on top of it to provide a wider surface, and remember that if your fuses are located there, the shrine and its contents will have to be moved to access them)
- In hanging baskets (wire or wicker; the three-tiered baskets make an interesting multilevel shrine)
- In a hanging pot rack (you can place bunches of dried flowers and other natural objects on top)

Here are some suggestions for items you may wish to include on your shrine or altar:

- Something to represent your connection to your ancestors
- Something to represent your household or hearth spirits

- Something to represent a hearth deity with whom you have a special connection or resonance, cultural or otherwise
- Something to represent the four elements (earth, air, fire, and water) or simply fire as a symbol of the spiritual hearth

Creating Images for Your Shrine

Rather than using found objects for your shrine, you can make images to represent the guardians or deities that you feel guide you in your kitchen. Or you can make representations of those entities and energies you wish to invoke in your hearth to attract more of the same or to be guiding lights.

For this project, you can use self-hardening clay, also known as air-drying clay, which does not require baking to set, or you can use heat-dried clay or another modeling substance. Work on a flat surface covered with plastic or newspaper to protect it from the clay.

Before you begin, decide what kind of shape or figure you wish to sculpt or form. It doesn't have to be a literal portrayal of the spirit or deity you feel drawn to; allow yourself to be inspired. Perhaps spend a few minutes with a pencil and paper doodling shapes or ideas for the figure. If you are making a figure to represent an abstract principle, again let your inspiration and instinct guide you.

The mint in this project is associated with abundance; the lavender is associated with peace; the cloves are associated with purification; the basil is associated with harmonious domestic management; the rosemary is associated with protection; the sage is associated with purification; and the salt is associated with purification and prosperity. These items were chosen for their general association with common themes in the practice of home-based spirituality. If there are other herbs whose energies are more appropriate to your chosen spirits or goal, use them instead.

You will need:

- Candle, candleholder
- Matches or lighter
- Self-hardening or heat-dried clay (about the size of your fist), color of your choice
- 1 pinch dried mint
- 1 pinch dried lavender
- 1 pinch ground cloves
- 1 pinch dried basil
- 1 pinch dried rosemary
- 1 pinch dried sage
- 1 pinch salt
- Small dish for herbs
- Tools to work the clay (toothpick, chopstick, skewer)
- Small dish of rice or salt

1. Take a moment to sit quietly and clear your mind. Take three deep breaths, releasing as much physical and mental tension as possible with each exhalation.
2. Light the candle, saying:

Sacred flame,
Bless my work with your light.

3. Knead the clay to soften it. As you knead, visualize the clay glowing with the energy of the deity, spirit, or principle you wish it to represent on your altar or shrine. Once it is soft, flatten it out with your hands.

4. Measure out the herbs and salt into the dish. Hold the dish in your hands and say,

Herbs,
I call forth your qualities of protection,
peace, harmony, purification, abundance, and prosperity.
May my hearth always be blessed by these,
and may those who live in this house know good fortune,
health, and love.

5. Hold the dish of herbs in front of the candle so that the light of the flame shines on them. Say:

Sacred flame,
Bless these herbs.

6. Sprinkle the herbs evenly over the flattened clay. Roll the clay up, then form it into a ball. Knead it again to distribute the herbs throughout the clay.

7. Begin to form the clay into a rough shape approximating your idea for the figure. When you have the basic shape, begin smoothing it. Add details with tools such as a toothpick, a chopstick, or a skewer.

8. Leave the figure in a safe place to dry. If it has very thick areas, the clay may need more time to dry out properly. Turn it at some point so that it dries evenly.

9. When the figure is dry, you may paint it or leave it as it is. (Check the packaging of the clay for suggestions regarding what kind of paint to use.)

10. Place the figure on your shrine. Place a small dish of salt, rice, olive oil, or some other kind of offering by it. In your own words, thank the deity, spirit, or principle for its blessings, and ask that it remain always by your hearth and bless your home.

Create Shrines Throughout the Home

The information regarding altars and shrines is applicable to any room in your house. If you are lucky enough to have a fireplace in your home, try using the mantelpiece as a shrine to the things you hold sacred. Photos of family, original artwork, candles, mirrors, colors and textures, statues or figurines all can be used to evoke a sense of your home and of your connection with the sacred principles in your life, as well as the Divine. Consider making it a family altar, with input from all members. Wherever the spiritual heart of your home is located, an altar or shrine can help confirm it and make it feel more real to you. All the suggestions here are easily applied or altered to create a shrine elsewhere in the home.

Shrines and altars don't need to be permanent. You can set one up for a specific event, for a period in your life, or for a season. They can be set up anywhere in the home. Denise Linn's beautiful book *Altars: Bringing Sacred Shrines Into Your Everyday Life* is an inspirational resource for this activity, as is Jean McMann's *Altars and Icons: Sacred Spaces in Everyday Life*. Both are illustrated in full color and demonstrate the wide variety of ways people collect, arrange, and situate sacred displays that reflect and honor certain ideals, principles, milestones, or loved ones.

Acting Mindfully in the Kitchen

If the kitchen is serving as the modern spiritual hearth, it stands to reason that any and all activity done in the room may qualify as having the potential for spiritual application. It's not as easy as declaring anything done within the kitchen as spiritual, however. While living one's life is a sacred undertaking, it's hard to argue that taking out the trash qualifies as spiritual. The key is to be in a spiritual headspace while performing certain tasks.

If we argue that every moment has the potential to be spiritual, then what is required is a method of initializing that potential and making it real. Performing an action with awareness (also known as acting mindfully) offers this possibility.

Doing something with awareness is also known as being fully within the moment. Being in the moment means not thinking about what has happened previous to the present or what you have to do next. It's granting the present task or situation your entire attention and focus and allowing it to unfold without forcing it or insisting that it occur in one way or another. Why is this considered a desirable thing? The main benefit of staying in the moment is that it engenders less stress. The position is relatively stress-free because there isn't an emphasis on "Oh no, I forgot to do something" or anxiety about what you have to do later, so it is more positive. This state is also more receptive to the healing and rejuvenating energy your spiritual hearth can provide. Being in the moment can help you appreciate the feel of your home and the impact your spiritual hearth has upon the people within it.

Perhaps the most important guiding principle for acting mindfully is to perform one task at a time. Multitasking is almost instinctive in today's world, but fight the drive to do as much as possible at once. You can't give your full attention to something if you're already dividing your attention between a number of tasks. By allowing yourself to focus on a single task, you are allowing yourself to absorb as much information as possible about it and opening yourself to the spiritual energies involved, maximizing the potential for benefit.

Being in the moment sounds easy. If you've ever tried it, however, it isn't as simple as it sounds. Here are some suggestions to help you be in the moment:

- **Be aware of your environment.** What sounds do you hear? What is the light like? What are the smells around you? This helps anchor you in the real world that is around you right now.

- **Be aware of yourself.** How does your physical body feel? What are the textures of the clothes against your skin? How do you feel internally on a physical level? What is your emotional state? Do not judge any of these things; simply accept them for what they are.
- **Imagine that you are seeing what is in front of you for the very first time.** Come at it with new eyes. Don't simply accept what you see; observe it and allow yourself to absorb the details instead of assuming that you know what is there because you see it every day.
- **Take at least three deep, slow breaths.** This is a commonly used technique to aid grounding, or reconnecting to the energy of the earth. It also features the bonus of delivering a good shot of oxygen to the lungs, which in turn oxygenates the blood.

It's impractical to consciously focus on every single move you make throughout the day as being spiritual. If you did, you'd likely go slightly mad under all the perceived pressure and repercussions. It's generally enough to touch base with your spiritual hearth once a day and ask that your actions be blessed throughout the day.

Make Some Moments Special

While it may be hard to make every action spiritual, you can mark certain actions or series of actions as consciously spiritual. Preparing a meal, for example, or tidying the kitchen are excellent examples of actions that can be consciously recognized as spiritual. It helps if you consciously assert this before each instance of the task. An excellent way to do this is to wash your hands. Water is considered a purifying element, apart from the basic physical association of cleaning with soap and water. Washing your hands with awareness makes an excellent trigger to signify the beginning of a spiritual act. It also provides a method of reconnecting to your spiritual hearth throughout the day, as it is a frequently performed action that can remind you to pause and reach out to engage with the power contained within your spiritual hearth, to restore or refresh yourself. Think of washing your hands as preparing yourself physically, emotionally, mentally, and spiritually for spiritual activity.

Here's an example of how to use washing your hands as a spiritual trigger.

1. Focus on being in the moment.
2. Turn the water on and let it run over your hands. Visualize the water washing away any negative or undesired energy.
3. Apply soap and wash your hands, keeping yourself in the moment. Notice how the soap feels on your skin, what the sensation of soapy skin over soapy skin feels like.
4. Rinse the soap off. Take three deep, slow breaths, releasing any tension or stress you may be holding as you exhale.
5. Dry your hands with a clean cloth.

If you like, you can say a small prayer that you create yourself or speak from the heart as you wash your hands.

By performing these steps with awareness and acknowledging that washing your hands is a spiritual act, you are signaling to your conscious and subconscious minds that you consider what you are about to do as important.

This is an excellent way to begin and end your day, as well. It provides you with an opportunity to be quiet and still for a moment and to acknowledge the sanctity of the spiritual heart of your home. It is a moment of honoring it with respect and honoring yourself as an integral element of that hearth. Doing it at the beginning of the day is a way to approach the day with openness and thanksgiving; doing it last thing at night before you turn off the kitchen light is a way to quietly thank your hearth.

Bringing Spirituality to Your Kitchen

Part of the trick to maintaining a home-based spiritual practice is to remind yourself frequently that your everyday life is a spiritual activity. The best way to do this is to establish a certain set of rituals to perform every day—some domestic activities that are set apart as ceremonial in some way and done with awareness and intent, not full-fledged ceremonial rituals in your kitchen. (Although if you want to do something like that, then go right ahead!) Regular tasks such as making coffee or setting the table are great opportunities to link a spiritual thought or act. It doesn't have to be complicated; it can be as basic as using the task to remind yourself that what you are doing is spiritual, just as everything else you do during the day and night is spiritual.

Here are some suggestions for what you can do to add more spiritual awareness to your kitchen-based activities.

- **Meditate:** Meditation can be as simple as sitting down in a tidied kitchen (or at least one free of crumbs, juice spills, and a stack of dishes in the sink) with a cup of tea, doing a series of body-relaxing exercises, and then just opening yourself up to the energy of the room and your home. You can choose something to think about or just let your mind drift.

- **Make offerings:** If you have a kitchen altar or shrine, touch base with it at least once a day. Offerings don't have to be big affairs; a pinch of an herb you're using to season a stew, a candle, even just a touch and a whispered "Thank you for being here" can do the trick.

- **Make housework spiritual by recognizing the sacred in the tasks:** If you're washing the dishes or mopping the floor, think about scrubbing the negativity away to reveal a pure and free object behind. Think of sweeping the kitchen like sweeping a temple: a clean place of worship or honoring is done out of respect for the deity or principle you're honoring.

- **Prepare food with awareness:** Instead of throwing something together for a meal, take the time to be in the moment as you assemble it. (There's more on this in Chapter 9.)

- **Consume food with awareness:** Some of us may associate saying grace before a meal with parental discipline, but it's a lovely idea. One such example is the Japanese Shinto practice of taking a moment before eating to thank the people who raised, harvested, transported, and were otherwise involved with getting the food from its natural state to your table. Even if it's a simple "Bless the hands that touched this food," a phrase like this spoken in quiet thanks provides you with a moment to reconnect with the world around you and the energy it emits.

- **Wipe counters:** When you wipe counters down at night, think of clearing away all the clutter of thoughts and events that happened during the day, leaving both your hearth and your mind calm and balanced.

- **Light a candle:** There is something very calming and spiritual about lighting a candle. It's a particularly fitting act for someone practicing hearthcraft, as the flame symbolizes so much about the practice. Try choosing a special candleholder and placing it on your kitchen shrine or somewhere particular in your kitchen, and lighting it before you begin work. Keep safety in mind when you choose where to place it. As you light it, visualize or speak aloud a welcome to the essence of the flame and the blessing it bestows upon your hearth. If a candle isn't your thing or you want to try something different, see the following section on oil lamps.

Lamps and Sacred Flames in the Kitchen

As the flame is one of the most common representations of the sacred, particularly in hearth-related spiritual paths, lighting a candle or some other kind of flame is a natural thing to do when you wish to have a physical representation of your spiritual hearth in the kitchen. As mentioned in Chapter 2, an eternal flame is used by many temples, churches, and shrines to signify the presence of the Divine.

Candles are lovely but need to be replaced on a frequent basis, and the heat of the kitchen as well as the drafts created by heat moving can make them burn unevenly or can even damage the candle, depending on where you place it. Additionally, the open flame may make you nervous. A good solution to these problems is to use an oil-burning lamp, such as a hurricane lamp or some variation of it (also known as kerosene lamps or paraffin lamps). Lamps like this are fueled by liquid oil that is contained within the base. A wick of cloth or other fiber runs from the oil up through the neck of the lamp, and the flame burns at the tip of the wick. Fuel is constantly drawn up the wick through capillary action. Usually the flame of an oil lamp is protected by a glass chimney, which allows the light to be seen and cast out into the room while protecting the flame from drafts. The height of the flame may be adjusted by turning a small screw that raises and lowers the wick, increasing or decreasing the amount of wick exposed above the fuel in the base.

There is another style of lamp that is sometimes referred to as an Aladdin lamp but is more correctly called a *dipa*. A *dipa* (literally "lamp") is a Hindu oil lamp made from a roughly oval clay dish or bowl with one elongated end forming a small open spoutlike channel in which is laid a wick formed of twisted cotton that draws the oil in the bowl up to feed the flame burning at the other end of the wick at the edge of the spout. There is often a handle at the other end of the oval. *Dipas* in temples can be impressive brass candelabra-shaped affairs holding these shallow dishes where candles would be placed, a wick burning in each one. *Dipa*-style lamps burning olive or other thick oils do not catch fire if tipped; the oil simply spreads and the flame dies.

The simplest kind of oil lamp can be made from any heat-safe dish and a wick from thin cotton string. Cut a piece of string about three inches long and tie a knot in the middle of it. Trim the string until there is an inch on one side and approximately a half-inch on the other. Take a small piece of tinfoil about a quarter-inch square, make a small hole in it with a thumbtack or pushpin, and thread the knotted string through it so that the knot rests on top. Bend the corners of the foil up slightly to make a dish shape. Float the square of foil on the top of the oil in the dish, knot side up. Wait a few minutes to allow the string to absorb oil, then light it. Trim this wick as necessary to avoid smoking and to obtain the best flame.

Create Your Own Lamp

You can create a lamp out of any kind of container made from nonflammable material. Making your own lamp provides you with the opportunity to design it to reflect the spiritual goals you'll be using it for. Try making your own dish out of clay, shaping it into whatever style or shape you desire or feel inspired to mold. Dry it, glaze it to seal the inside surface, and fire it in a kiln. (Check your city's listings for ceramic groups or shops that can provide this service or that can help you make the dish on site. Local schools may also offer evening workshops or classes.)

You can experiment with the following materials to find the perfect wick for your homemade lamp. In all cases, be certain that your material is 100 percent cotton and not blended with anything:

- Waxed candle wicks (make sure there's no metal wire inside)
- Spools of braided round or square wicking for candles
- Cotton batting, loosely twisted into a wick-like shape
- Cotton kitchen string

Make sure to use a saucer or dish under the lamp if you're using one that has a wick lying against the lip of the container; the capillary action that feeds the wick can leak oil over the edge.

Oil Lamps and the Divine

Lighting an oil lamp when you work in the kitchen is a lovely way to signify that you are aware of the presence of the Divine. You can light this before each session in the kitchen or first thing each morning. Safety indicates that you should extinguish it before you leave the house. As you do, say a prayer or something as simple as "Although I extinguish the physical flame, the spiritual flame continues to burn both at the shrine and in my heart." Say this each time you extinguish the flame and say something similar when you relight it when you return to the kitchen, such as "I physically relight this sacred flame, reflecting the spiritual flame that burns continually at this shrine and in my heart."

When lighting it first thing in the morning, a more involved prayer is appropriate. Something along these lines, for example:

Sacred flame, symbol of purity and life,
I light you now and invoke your sanctity.
Descend upon the members of this household, and upon this room.
Bless every person who enters it.
Grant us peace, health, protection, and joy.
I thank you for your many blessings, sacred flame.

At the end of the day, extinguish the flame. This is associated with the traditional smooring of the hearth, the banking of the coals and embers to keep them alive but protected so that a fire could be easily built and lit the next morning (see Chapter 2). A prayer such as the following can be said:

Sacred flame, symbol of purity and life,
I extinguish your physical form, although never your sanctity.
We are grateful for your many blessings.
Keep our family and home safe throughout the night.
I thank you for your many blessings, sacred flame.

Tending to Your Lamp

The oil lamp provides you with a visible reminder of the spiritual hearth. Tending the lamp can be a satisfying act that engages you with physical activity while serving a spiritual function. Here are some things you'll need to consider for the care and functioning of your lamp.

The basic fuel used for oil lamps is kerosene, a clear, thin water-like liquid with a slightly greasy feel to it. It is usually sold in two forms: kerosene and paraffin oil. Pure paraffin oil is a refined kerosene that burns with very little soot and odor, making it a good choice for indoor wick lamps. (It is not a liquid form of paraffin wax.) Always use the purest form of oil that you can afford or find to minimize airborne by-products that may be hazardous to your health. Never use other fuels or oils that are not designated for use indoors, as the fumes created may be toxic. Avoid buying colored or scented lamp oils, as the fumes from the burning additives that lend the color and scent may not be as safe to breathe. Keep any oil lamp out of the reach of children, as well as the fuel.

In general, the thinner oils with a water–like consistency or viscosity work best in closed hurricane lamps, while thicker oils like olive and castor work better in *dipa*–style lamps.

An oil lamp that burns olive oil is a particularly appropriate piece of equipment for this purpose, as opposed to an oil lamp that burns paraffin. Why use fossil fuel when you can burn a plant-based oil that is likely already in your kitchen?

Additionally, the burning of the oil can be seen as an offering, which ties together the oil lamp and the idea of offerings made to the spirits of the hearth nicely. Olive oil is of a thicker viscosity than kerosene, and the capillary action that draws the kerosene up the wick in a hurricane lamp is not strong enough to draw thicker oils to feed the flame. Therefore, if you are looking to use a thicker oil as a fuel for a presence flame, consider the *dipa* or dish-based style of lamp.

Be vigilant about keeping the wick trimmed so that the oil does not gum up the wick and slow down or stop capillary action. Olive oil is shipped from many miles away, and for that reason you may object to it on an ethical basis for the transportation and fuel expended in bringing it to you. Other vegetable oils can be used as fuel for lamps as well with varying degrees of success and brightness of flame, such as coconut oil, castor oil, palm oil, and sweet almond oil. Clarified butter was used as a lamp oil in India, as Hindu culture holds the cow as sacred, and thus offerings of dairy products were often made.

Chapter 7

Using Hearthcraft to Protect Your Home

ONE OF THE MAIN FOCI OF HEARTH MAGIC revolves around protection, both of persons and possessions. The home is the root of your family's energy and spirituality. If you are working to honor and strengthen it, and to make it as peaceful and spiritually nourishing as possible for you and your family, it only makes sense to protect it from harm or attack. Protection and purification are two of the most important concepts in home-based spirituality. This chapter focuses on how to maintain a clear and balanced energy within the home, how to cleanse and purify the atmosphere, how to handle threats, and how to build up magical defenses.

Protecting Your Home on a Spiritual Level

Common sense dictates that you defend your home physically by using secure locks, high fences with locking gates, security systems, locking windows, and so forth. Once this is done, however, there are many other things you can do to protect your home on a spiritual level.

Keeping track of your home's energy is important. The best way to do this is to be familiar with your home's regular energy, to be better able to identify shifts or changes or problem areas that need to be dealt with. Being aware of your home's energy is crucial. Being familiar with its natural fluctuations, its cycles and responses to natural and environmental stimuli, is an important factor in identifying and handling disruptions and problems.

Make a point of knowing every corner of your home, even (or perhaps especially) areas you don't frequent, such as storage areas, garage corners, the attic, and so forth. Don't forget the crawl space, if your home has one, or partial attics accessible through trapdoors or hatches in the ceiling of a closet somewhere. If you have a shed or outbuilding built onto the side or back of the house, get to know its energy as well. Physically walking through these areas allows you to touch their energies with your own, which in turn gives you a better sense of what they feel like and allows you to interact directly with the energy there.

Evaluate Your Home's Energy

This is an exercise that you can do to get a good overall sense of what your home's energy is like. It is a good idea to do this exercise yearly or more frequently if your home is in a busy neighborhood, if you have a lot of people moving in and out, or if you experience a lot of emotional upheaval.

First make a list of all the rooms and connecting spaces in and directly adjacent to your home. Physically walk through the house and make note of all these places. Doing the physical tour will help you see and remember all the little places you might otherwise forget. You might list the major rooms in your home off the top of your head—kitchen, living room, bedrooms, bathroom—but if you walk from one to another you may realize that you've forgotten the hallway, the stairs up to the second floor, or the entryway between the front door and the hall, among other places.

Don't forget storage cupboards, pantries, and linen closets either. All these spaces are separate and serve separate functions. If you have an open-plan home or a large room that is separated into zones by function such as a family room that has a desk, a craft table for sewing, and a TV area, break the room down into those zones on your list (write down "family room: TV," "family room: sewing area"). It's important to understand the function each room in your house serves because it affects the energy produced and held within the room. A mismatch between the room's envisioned function and the purpose it actually serves can create a skewed energy too; exploring this can help you refocus the energy in your rooms and remove what negatively affects the desired energy.

Make a chart like this:

1. Room name:
2. Date:
3. Adjacent rooms:
4. Cardinal position:
5. Use:
6. Energy observations:
7. Suggestions or recommendations:
8. Miscellaneous:

When you've got your list, pick a room and go back to it. Go through the chart item by item and make your notes.

Room Name and Date

This sounds obvious, but you're going to be keeping these notes to refer to later, and while things may seem fresh in your mind now, I guarantee that after you've done this you won't necessarily remember when you did it. After the date, write down the weather, moon phase, day of the week, time of day, or any other associated information that you think interesting or that you believe may affect the energy readings you will take. This is as much a way to evaluate how you interact with your home's energy as it is an assessment of the house energy itself. It can be helpful later to go through these papers and realize that you can't do a clear energy evaluation when the moon is full, for example.

Adjacent Rooms and Cardinal Position

When you write your notes, don't forget to include what rooms are above and below the room you are in. The energy of these rooms impacts the room's energy as well. The cardinal position helps further situate the location. Does the room face west or northeast? This can be important if there is something such as a large shopping mall or a body of water in one direction or another. These things have large fields of energy that can affect your home as well and often have a greater effect on the rooms closer to them. When you're done, look at what rooms adjoin one another and see what kinds of energy are interacting through the wall or floor. If you live in an apartment, chances are good your next-door neighbor isn't going to allow you into his or her home to "sense the energy" of the room adjoining your wall. Apartments are a different kettle of fish. Assume the energy on the other side is on the bad side of neutral and create wards and shields accordingly. Better to be safe than sorry.

Use

What is this room used for? Rooms have an interesting habit of adapting to a family's needs, and the original use of the room is often modified as the family's needs change. First, list what it is supposed to be used for (library? den? office? playroom?). Then list what actually happens in the room (video games? TV watching? ironing? homework?). Sometimes the energy in a room is more conducive to something else rather than what you slated it to be when you moved in.

Energy Observations

How does the room feel to you? If you walk into the middle of it and close your eyes, how does it affect you emotionally? Do you feel relaxed? Tense? Angry? Sleepy? Now open your eyes and sense how it feels to you with the added visual information. Write both down. Walk through the room and see if your feelings change from location to location. Within the overall energy of a room there are very often several pockets of energy stronger in one sense than another. Draw a rough map of these energy sensings.

Suggestions or Recommendations

These can be spiritual, magical, or physical in nature. Should you move the furniture around? Remove a piece? Add a piece? Change the color scheme? Switch the room with another to make better use of the energies in each location? Should you add a certain elemental energy to balance an excess or lack of a certain element? Is an immediate purification indicated to cleanse the energy of something negative?

Miscellaneous

Use this category to write down anything that doesn't fit somewhere else. Is there something in the room that needs repair? A reminder you want to set for yourself? Look back over your notes. You should have what is in essence a snapshot of your home's energy as it stands at the present moment. This reference can be used as a baseline when you sense something odd or different in your home.

Set Up Energy Boundaries

Setting up energy barriers or boundaries is a good way not only to keep track of what is happening with your home's energy at all times but also to control what kind of energy comes into it. The threshold is a logical place to encode with a spiritual barrier. As the natural entrance and egress to your home, it can serve as a filter or blockade for undesired energy. Windows also should be protected, as they make easy alternatives to doors.

Threshold Protection Ritual

The threshold is a magical place, as it is neither in the house nor out, and yet it is part of both. Using the threshold as a focus for a protective spell is a first defense. This ritual not only cleanses the threshold; it also empowers it to function as a filter to allow positive energy into the home while keeping negative or disruptive energy out.

This creates a protective barrier keyed to the threshold of your house. If you have more than one entrance you use regularly, perform this ritual at the entrance you use more frequently, then at the secondary entrance.

You will need:

- 1 cup water
- ½ cup vinegar
- 1 tablespoon salt
- 1 tablespoon lemon juice
- Bowl or bucket
- Washing cloth

- Sage smudge (or loose dried sage)
- Matches or lighter
- Censer or heatproof dish
- Sealing oil (see Chapter 11, or use a tablespoon of olive oil with a pinch of salt added to it)
- 3 cloves garlic

1. Blend the water, vinegar, salt, and lemon juice together in a bowl or bucket. With the cloth, use this mixture to wash the threshold and doorframe. Be thorough: scrub the threshold inside and out, as well as the doorframe on both sides of the door, and both sides of the door itself.

2. Light the sage smudge and move it around the doorframe, wafting the smoke so that it touches the area inside and out. Lay the smudge in a censer or heatproof dish and allow it to smolder while you complete the ritual.

3. Dip your finger in the sealing oil and draw an unbroken line around the outside of the doorframe. Dip your finger in the oil again as necessary, but begin again exactly where you left off or retrace an inch or so of the line to ensure its continuity. As you draw the line, say:

No evil or illness may cross this threshold.
I hereby bar it from entering.
My home is sacred, and protected.

4. Dip your finger in the oil again. On the inside of the doorframe, touch your finger to the upper left corner and trace a line in the air down and across the doorway to touch the lower right corner. Dip your finger in the oil again, touch it to the upper right corner, and draw a line in the air down and across to touch the lower left corner. Dip your finger one last time and touch it to the middle of the lintel above the door and draw a line in the air straight down to touch the middle of the threshold. As you do so, say again:

No evil or illness may cross this threshold.
I hereby bar it from entering.
My home is sacred, and protected.

This symbol is a hexefus, or a combination of the runes Isa (a vertical line) and Gebo (an X). Gebo represents exchanges of energy or material objects, while Isa represents a static state (it translates to "ice"). Drawn together in this bindrune form, Isa "freezes" the state of your home and possessions, protecting it from physical and other intrusion.

5. Take three cloves of garlic. Touch each of them with a finger dipped in the oil. Bury them under your threshold or doorstep or as near to it as possible. Bury one at each end of the step or threshold, and one in the middle. As you do so, say again one final time:

No evil or illness may cross this threshold.
I hereby bar it from entering.
My home is sacred, and protected.

If you like, you can adapt this ritual and apply it to your windows as well. Bury a single clove of garlic in the ground under each window.

Wards

A ward is something that protects or defends. When used in connection with a house or home "to ward something" is to set up an autonomous system of protection.

> A word of advice about wards and protective barriers: if you're keeping something out, you're also keeping something in at the same time. It's healthy to lower wards and barriers now and again to allow what you've trapped inside to move around and air the place out, so to speak.

The caveat is that you have to check on your ward regularly. Just like raising a wall around a city to defend it, if you don't take a regular walk around and look at the state of the wall you've built, it can crumble, grow weak, be affected by the weather or vines. You can't just raise it and ignore it; it needs to be refreshed now and again. How often depends on the kind of neighborhood you live in.

Constructing a Ward

This is a good basic ward for your home. It needs frequent renewal. Two or four times a year is good; try tying it to the seasonal shifts. If you feel the ward has been compromised in

some way, take it down (see the next section) and reconstruct
it afresh.

You will need:

- Candle in a candleholder
- Matches or lighter
- Dish of water
- Dish of earth (you may use salt, but as you will be sprinkling
  this on the ground, it's not advisable)
- Incense (your choice)
- Censer

1. Light the candle. Beginning at your threshold, walk around the
    outside of your dwelling, carrying the candle in front of you.
    As you walk, say:

    I build this boundary with fire.

2. Repeat the sentence as you walk all the way around the
    building. Visualize the path the flame traces hanging in the air
    as a band of energy. When you return to your threshold, set
    down the candle.

3. Pick up the dish of water and walk around the building again,
    dipping your fingers into the water and sprinkling it as you
    walk. As you do, say:

    I build this boundary with water.

4. Repeat the sentence as you walk all the way around the
    building. Visualize the path the water traces hanging in the air

as a band of energy. When you return to your threshold, set down the dish of water.

5. Pick up the dish of earth and walk around the building again, dipping your fingers into the earth and sprinkling it as you walk. As you do, say:

    I build this boundary with earth.

6. Repeat the sentence as you walk all the way around the building. Visualize the path the earth traces hanging in the air as a band of energy. When you return to your threshold, set down the dish of earth.

7. Light the incense and place it in the censer. Pick it up and walk around the building again, wafting the smoke around you as you walk. As you do, say:

    I build this boundary with air.

8. Repeat the sentence as you walk all the way around the building. Visualize the path the smoke traces hanging in the air as a band of energy. When you return to your threshold, set down the censer.

9. Standing at your threshold, reach out with your hands as if you were placing your palms on a wall. Visualize the four circuits you made with the elements fusing together, expanding into a solid wall of energy. Then visualize that wall of energy growing down into the ground and curving in until it meets under your dwelling. Visualize the top growing up and in until it meets overhead, thus forming a sphere of energy enclosing the building. Say:

Fire, water, earth, and air,

Guard this home against all ill will and danger.

Keep this house and those who live in it safe.

I declare this ward to be raised and active.

Removing a Ward

Sometimes a ward must be dismantled. If you move, for example, or if your home energy changes significantly in some way (the addition of a new member of the family or lodger, for example, a major change in career, or a physical alteration of the house through renovation or addition), the original ward, programmed to recognize and protect a certain energy and home entity, can become less effective. Dissolving it or taking it down is a smart step before rebuilding a new ward. Rather than trying to reshape and adapt what you originally put up, release the energy of the ward and start afresh. Building on the old ward is inadvisable because it has its foundations in something that technically no longer exists.

Dissolving an Existing Ward

To dissolve an existing ward, begin at your threshold and walk counterclockwise around your dwelling. As you do, hold your hand out with the palm down and visualize it slicing through the wall or boundary you constructed when you raised the ward. As you walk, say:

I dissolve this ward.

You have my thanks for your protection in the past.

I release you with my blessing.

When you return to your threshold, stamp your foot on it to shake loose the ties to any remaining energy of the past ward and say,

I declare this ward dissolved.

Plants, Stones, and Other Protective Techniques

You can also use the energies of living plants and trees as well as natural stones to protect your home.

Trees and Plants

One of the easiest things to do to protect your house is to plant trees, shrubs, and plants associated with defense and protection around it. If you're thinking of planting a tree on your property, you can choose one that has protective associations, thereby extending the tree's value to your home and land as well. If you already have one of these trees on your land or near your home, introduce yourself to it and thank it for the energy it emanates.

- **Hawthorn:** protects against damage from storms, encourages happiness
- **Birch:** protects children
- **Rowan:** protects health
- **Hazel:** protects against evil; encourages abundance and inspiration
- **Oak:** defends against physical harm

- **Sassafras:** defends from evil spirits
- **Elder:** defends against evil and negative energy
- **Lilac:** defends against harmful spirits

When you plant a tree for protection, you can say a prayer such as the following:

Sacred tree [or bush],
Grant us your protection.
May your roots defend us against harm from below,
May your branches defend us against harm from above.
May your leaves and shade
Extend your protection to our home and property.
In return we will care for you, sacred tree,
And guard you against blight and drought.
Sacred tree, we welcome you to our family.

If you don't own land but there is an existing tree nearby that you wish to use as part of your house and home protection, introduce yourself to it by spending time sitting with it. Get to know its energy and decide if you wish to incorporate it into your work. Trees, like other natural objects, are living creatures and may or may not feel open to working with you. After getting to know its energy over a few days, offer the tree water and ask it if it is willing to work with you as a home guardian. Trust your intuition for the answer.

Using Stones for Protection

Stones and gems are frequently used as protective objects for their associated energies and qualities. These stones in particular are good to use in the home:

- **Amber:** health, prevents energy drain, transforms negative energy to positive energy
- **Amethyst:** absorbs negative energy, promotes harmony
- **Apache tear:** encourages harmony in times of stress
- **Aventurine:** defends prosperity and health
- **Carnelian:** success, creativity, protection from nightmares, equalizes emotions such as anger and grief
- **Hematite:** reflects negativity
- **Jade:** wisdom, fidelity
- **Lapis lazuli:** harmony, serenity
- **Malachite:** prosperity, abundance, protection
- **Obsidian:** absorbs negative energy
- **Onyx:** happiness, good luck
- **Quartz crystal:** transforms negative energy to positive, source of energy for those in the home
- **Rose quartz:** transforms negative energy into positive energy, encourages affection
- **Tiger eye:** stability, wealth

Other Protective Techniques

Folk magic and cultural customs are a treasure trove of protective techniques. Here are some to consider:

- Paint magical symbols on walls/ceilings for a specific purpose, using salt water or lemon water. If you get the chance to do it before you repaint a room, do it in the same color of paint before you paint over it.
- Walk your property boundaries with cornmeal and water (separately), asking blessings and friendship of the spirits of the land to guard and protect those who live here.
- Salt water left out in the center of a room all night will absorb negativity. Wash it away with flowing water in the sink or outdoors the next morning.
- Placing a mirror in a window on each side of your home, facing outward, will reflect negativity back to the sender. Likewise hanging a witch ball (a polished glass globe) in the window will absorb and return negative energy.
- Bells or wind chimes hung from the doors guard against intruders and stagnant energy. Hang them where the air currents can ring them. They will set up movement in the air and clear the psychic energy of your home.
- Hang a mirror empowered to reflect negative energy inside, facing the front door.
- Bury protective stones such as onyx, malachite, or amethyst under your doorstep, porch, or steps.
- Wash your doorstep with purifying wash (see Chapter 11).
- Hang Pennsylvania Dutch hex signs associated with protection inside and outside your house.
- Hang an iron horseshoe above your door, with the open end facing upward.

Purifying and Cleansing Your Home

To maintain your home's balanced energy, establish a set number of times throughout the year to do cleansings, purifications, and blessings. They don't all have to be major undertakings: like physical housework, the more often you do it, the lighter the workload is each time.

You may choose to vary the schedule. For example, you may do a major deep purification twice a year (on the solstices, perhaps), with minor purifications on the first day of each month or at each full or dark moon. Or you may choose to do a regular mid-level cleansing and blessing on each sabbat or bank holiday. Choose a time that will work for you and blend into your schedule with the least amount of awkwardness. If you prefer your spiritual or energy work to be associated with moon phases or holy days, schedule your house purifications around those times. Then decide if you will do it before the date in order to have your house cleansed and ready to experience the energy of the day in question, if you will do your work on the day itself to take advantage of the associated energy for your purification, or if you will do the work directly following the day in order to have a clean slate for the energies of the next section of the cycle. Alternately, perhaps you function best on a regular calendar-type schedule; planning a regular purification on the same date every month will help you keep the rhythm.

There is no right or wrong way. Do what makes sense to you and what feels right. The point is to do it regularly, as regularly as your space requires and your schedule allows.

The frequency of purification and cleansing depends on the energy of your home, which is one of the reasons the previous evaluation exercise was suggested. If your home sees heavy traffic from visitors or heavy emotional situations, it may be best to purify more often than if you live alone.

You may find that certain rooms respond better to specific techniques. That's fine. Use the technique that works best in the room you're purifying. It may be a bit more work to switch techniques if you're doing a full house purification, but in the long run it's best for the overall energy of the home. The point is to be as effective and efficient as possible, and while changing techniques may take a bit more time, it promotes a smoother household, which in turn affects everything done inside it.

Purification Techniques

There are dozens of ways to purify a room of unwanted energy. But first, let's talk about negative energy versus unwanted energy. There are times when an energy is positive but not wanted in a specific place. For example, energy that soothes and promotes sleep is a positive kind of energy, but it is not desirable in a home office where you want to be alert and productive. Of course, the unwanted energy may be negative as well.

Generally you'll strive for as positive an environment as possible in your home. However, there are also energies that can be classified as "neutral through positive" that for some reason may not be suitable for the atmosphere you are seeking to create in a specific space. For this reason, the term *banishing* isn't used here. Banishing something creates a vacuum of sorts, an empty space that must and will be filled with something else. If you consciously banish something, then logic dictates that you should be prepared to consciously replace it with positive energy. But banishing neutral through positive energy doesn't make sense, and for that reason the terms *transform* or *reprogram* are more appropriate.

If the negative energy is occupying a space that has a natural positive vibration to it, then absorbing or removing the negative energy will generally result in the return of the natural positive balance.

Some of the following techniques are more active than others. For example, smudging with chosen herbs is a more active process than leaving a sliced onion in a room to absorb unwanted energy.

While at heart most of these techniques address the removal of negative energy, most can be consciously programmed to affect other energies as well.

Sage and Herb Smudging

Many cultures employ a technique of purifying via smoke created by burning plant matter considered sacred or honored in some way. Incense is one such example. Smudging with sage is a Native American technique that has proven very adaptable and effective for people of any tradition and spiritual path. Essentially, a bundle of dried herbs is lit and the flame is extinguished, leaving the dry plant matter to smolder and produce a smoke that has the qualities of the plant matter itself. This smoke is easily wafted around a room or other space, can insinuate into nooks and crannies, and has the ability to surround objects. It is also less likely to damage objects, whereas water or flame (two of the other popularly recognized purifiers) can damage things. The bundle of herbs is referred to as a smudge or a smudge stick and is easily carried in the hand. The act of surrounding someone or something with the smoke is called smudging. Smudging may also be done by crumbling dried plant matter on a charcoal tablet.

Sage is the original and most popular herb to use in this respect, but there are other popular herbs commonly used such as cedar, sweetgrass, and lavender. These four herbs generally encourage a calm atmosphere with positive energy. Sage and cedar in particular are considered sacred herbs in the Native American traditions.

There's no right or wrong way to make a smudge stick, but here's a general guideline.

To make a smudge:

1. Lay several dried stalks of your chosen herb(s) together.
2. Slip a length of natural undyed cotton string under one end of the bundle and begin wrapping the stalks, crisscrossing the string over and under the bundle, tying it at various intervals. Wrap it firmly but not so tightly that the stalks are completely crushed together; air needs

to circulate through the bundle in order to maintain the smoldering process.

3. Tie the ends of the string firmly at the other end of the bundle. Wrapping and tying the smudge in this way allows the bundle to stay tied when you begin burning it and when the string at the end burns through. Don't worry if bits of the dried herb break off as you wrap the smudge.

Other things to remember when making a smudge:

- Stalks that are too thick will not burn well; stalks that are too thin will snap when you wrap the bundle.
- Don't make a bundle that is more than 1½" in diameter once it's wrapped and tied; it will be difficult to keep smoldering.
- A smudge smaller than ½" may be too fragile.
- If you prefer, you may harvest your own fresh herbs and wrap them while fresh, then hang the bundle up in a well-ventilated place to dry thoroughly. The bundle must be completely dry before you use it, or it will not burn properly. Watch it carefully during the drying process to ensure that the bundle does not grow mildew.

How to Use a Smudge

When you smudge, do so with awareness, sensitivity, and respect for the act while visualizing your goal. You may say a short prayer or invocation before beginning or not, as you feel necessary. Something as simple as "Sage (or whatever single herb or combination of herbs you are using), I call upon your sacred energy to cleanse this space" can work. Light one end of the smudge by touching it to a flame and make sure the smudge has caught well before gently blowing the flame out. The ends of the dry herbs should still glow red and give off smoke. Air needs to move through the smudge to keep it smoldering, and you can facilitate this by fanning the smoke gently with your free hand. This movement also allows you to direct the smoke into corners and around objects. You may also use a feather. If you carry the smudge around the room in your hand, bits of burning plant matter will fall onto the floor. Smudges are often laid in a heatproof container such as a shell, earthenware bowl (unglazed ceramic or clay works well), or a rock with a depression in it, to catch these bits.

> Smudging may also be used to purify an object before use or to clear accumulated energy from a tool.

The entire smudge need not be used. You can extinguish it in a bowl of salt or sand, making extremely certain that it has completely gone out, and wrap it in aluminum foil or store it in a paper bag until your next smudging.

Burning Incense

Like smudging, burning incense releases smoke that carries the energy of the incense's ingredients. The point of this is to get that energy moving around in an easily dispersible way. You could sprinkle the actual herbs around, but gravity will probably make it difficult to access higher pockets of the energy you're trying to move.

You can use preprepared incense from a retailer in a scent or formula specifically prepared for purification, or you can use a pure scent that is associated with purification. Cedar, sage, lavender, and frankincense are single scents that are often used to purify; blends labeled "Purification" often include these. Preprepared incense usually comes in stick or cone form.

Stick incense can be made in one of two ways: rolled (a wet mixture of ingredients is rolled into a thin cylinder and dried, sometimes around a thin stick to give it support) or dipped (a blank stick with a neutral paste molded around it is dipped into a solution of oils). Cone incense, like rolled incense, is made from a paste of ingredients, then shaped. Sticks and cones are usually self-combustible, meaning they do not require a charcoal tablet to burn them. By lighting the end of a stick or cone, waiting until the tip glows red, then gently blowing out the flame, the incense will burn on its own. Sticks and cones are convenient and do not require anything other than a bowl with salt or sand in which to burn them and catch the ashes, although censers (also known as incense burners) are easy to find. Censers for sticks are usually long curved flat pieces of stone or wood, with tiny holes at one end into which the sticks are inserted, which hold the stick at an angle so the ash falls onto the burner.

Loose Incense

Loose incense is literally that: a blend of roughly ground or chopped plant matter and/or resin that must be burned on a charcoal tablet in order to release its energy in the form of smoke. This is the easiest kind to make at home, and it can be made in almost any proportion, mostly from ingredients in your pantry or spice cabinet.

Here are some commonly found kitchen herbs that you can use in a purifying incense:

- Cinnamon
- Clove
- Rosemary
- Sage
- Thyme

You can also find things in your garden like lavender and rose, which you can dry and then add to the incense. Alternatively, you can use the essential oil of any of these ingredients and add a couple of drops to the dry ingredients and mix it all together well.

Burning dry herbs never smells like the essential oil or the dry herb itself in a bottle. In fact, it can smell pretty much like burning leaves or grass, which isn't always pleasant. To offset the burning-leaf smell you can add resins, as resins tend to have a sweeter smell than dried plant matter does. You'll have to purchase resins like the following, but they can really make your incense extra special:

- Frankincense
- Benzoin
- Golden copal

To test the incense, you'll need a charcoal tablet and a bowl filled with salt or sand in which to burn it. Light the charcoal tablet by holding the edge of it to a flame. (Be careful; it can ignite quickly. You may want to use tweezers or small tongs to hold it safely.) When the charcoal begins to spark, put it down in the salt- or sand-filled bowl. When the sparks have finished traveling across the surface of the tablet and the charcoal begins to glow red in patches, it is ready. Take a pinch of your incense and place it on the charcoal. Observe how it reacts so that you'll be prepared for it when you first use it in a larger quantity. Don't put more than a teaspoon of loose incense on the charcoal tablet at a time, or you may smother the charcoal as well as have to open a window to clear some of the smoke! It's a good idea to have an extra bowl of sand to dump on top of the charcoal tablet if you need to extinguish it quickly. Be careful; sometimes charcoal will continue to smolder. To make sure it's really out, pour water over it.

Purifying Incense

Blending your own purifying incense means you're using exactly the kind of energies you want to use in your house. And when you do it with clear intent and awareness, you're adding an extra dimension of personal energy to the process, keying it to your home and family and spiritual practice. Here's a basic recipe for loose purifying incense.

You will need:

- 1 teaspoon frankincense resin
- 1 teaspoon copal resin

- Mortar and pestle
- Small bottle or jar with lid
- ½ teaspoon dried lavender
- ½ teaspoon rosemary
- Pinch ground cloves

1. Place the frankincense and copal resin in the mortar. Gently crush the resin with the pestle. Transfer it to the jar. If there is any residue left in the mortar, scrape it out gently and add it to the jar. Resin tends to melt under enthusiastic grinding and can gum up the mortar. Be gentle, and don't feel that you have to reduce the fragments to powder. Chips that are smaller than the granules the resin arrived in is fine.
2. Place the lavender and rosemary in the mortar. Grind them into smaller pieces and transfer to the jar.
3. Add the pinch of ground cloves to the jar.
4. Cap the jar and gently shake it to combine all the ingredients.

Folk Techniques for Purifying

Tradition and folklore provide dozens of ways to clear bad luck, negative energy, bad feelings, and unwanted nasties from rooms and other places. Common and popular purification techniques include:

- Burning candles
- A slice of onion left on a saucer in the center of the room to absorb negative energy
- A slice of lemon left on a saucer in the center of the room to absorb negative energy

- A bowl of water left to absorb unwanted energy
- Stones programmed to absorb unwanted energy
- Asperging with salt water
- Asperging with herbal water (herbs left to soak in water for a specific time, drained, then dispersed via fingers or spray bottle)
- Sprinkling salt around a room (and vacuuming it up later)
- Sprinkling powdered or ground herbs around a room (and vacuuming it up later)
- Dispersing essential oil into the air via an aromatherapy jar
- Hanging strings of garlic or onions in the kitchen to absorb negative energy

Room Purification Ritual

It's important to note that terms such as *purify, cleanse,* and *bless* are often used interchangeably, but they do mean slightly different things.

- To *cleanse* something means to remove the physical dirt from it, with the intent to remove any associated energy influence.
- To *purify* something means to remove the negative or undesired energy from it.
- To *bless* something means to infuse the item with positive Divine-influenced or Divine-originated energy.

Basic Room Purification Ritual

This is an all-purpose purification ritual that can be used as is or as a basis for your own ritual.

You will need:

- Cleaning supplies (as needed)
- Incense (stick or loose) or smudge stick
- Charcoal tablet (if using loose incense)
- Censer or heatproof bowl
- Salt or sand (if using bowl for incense)
- Candle (white or color of your choice)
- Candleholder
- Matches or lighter

1. Begin by physically cleaning the space. Tidy the room. Put things in their place or return them to their original places in other rooms. Then vacuum, sweep, dust, polish—do whatever you need to do to remove physical dirt. It can be as thorough as you feel it needs to be.

2. Purify the room by burning a teaspoonful of your favorite purifying incense (or use the recipe in this chapter) on a charcoal tablet. Alternatively, use a stick of purchased incense in a purifying scent or use a smudge stick (homemade or purchased). As you light it say:

    I light this incense to purify this space.

3. Place the bowl or censer in the middle of the room and let the smoke fill the space. More incense is not necessarily

better; a single small spoonful can produce billows of smoke depending on the blend you're using. Make sure you test the blend beforehand. If you like, you can walk around the room in a counterclockwise direction to help disperse the smoke throughout the space. Counterclockwise movement is associated with banishing or undoing something.

4. Allow the incense to purify the room for as long as you feel it is necessary. It may take anywhere between a few minutes to a few hours. Don't worry about keeping the incense burning all that time; let the energies released with the original spoonful or stick do their work. If you sense that it will take longer than the initial burn time, check on the room or space after an hour (or after the incense has finished burning, or once the smoke has cleared) to evaluate whether you need to burn more incense or follow up with another purifying technique.

5. When the space feels purified, light the candle and place it in the middle of the space, saying:

    I light this flame to bless this space.

6. Allow it to burn down.

If you plan to purify a space for the first time, or for the first time in a long time, do all three of them in order. Begin by cleansing the room, then purify it, and finally ask Spirit or your concept of the Divine or your spiritual hearth to bless it. For the less intense maintenance rituals, you may choose to do the purification alone. For a touch of spiritual energy as the mood or desire strikes you, the blessing is ideal.

Energy Maintenance in Your Home

The term *order* suggests a specific arrangement, not just tidiness, and this is an essential part of keeping your home a harmonious place. The kind of energy created by the interaction of your furniture and possessions can be changed or otherwise affected by rearranging it or altering the contents of a room. Things possess energies of their own to different degrees, and together they create a larger collective energy. Adding things to the collective energy, or taking them away, can influence the feel of a room.

The flow of energy within a room is important. Often a room is unwelcoming because the energy within it doesn't flow; instead, it is stagnant. If you don't sense how this happens (either by deliberate energy sensing or a vague feeling concerning the room), try standing in the doorway to the room and looking in. Where are your eyes drawn right away? What path do they trace if you don't deliberately turn them in one direction or another? Chances are good that's the path the energy of the room takes too. If your eyes don't naturally move around the room, the energy probably doesn't either. If there's an area that is unused, despite having chairs or other furniture and equipment provided, the flow of energy through the room may not reach there, or it may be blocked by something.

To attract or encourage certain kinds of energy, place objects or symbols associated with that energy in key areas. This can be a major rearrangement or something unobtrusive. You can place small images that carry or represent desired energy in corners or nooks and crannies: a small image of a bee in a "dead" corner, for example, can help keep it vibrant, for the bee is a symbol of activity, community, and industry.

Chapter 8

Magic at the Hearth

IN HEARTHCRAFT, magic is a way of consciously drawing on the energy of the spiritual hearth to enhance the activity you are engaged in. In many paths magic and spiritual practices are separate, but in hearthcraft the magical activity both supports and draws from spiritual activity. As so much of hearthcraft revolves around love, nurturing, and protection of what you consider sacred, positive goals can be the only ones envisioned.

Another way of looking at magic within the context of hearthcraft is as transformation of some kind, a task performed with the intent to weave together energies in order to initiate some sort of spiritual transformation, rejuvenation, or growth. With that in mind, this chapter looks at kitchen folklore and customs and the energies associated with the equipment found and used in the kitchen.

The Magic in Everyday Objects

The materials you work with all possess their own energies. Here's a look at the common materials found in the kitchen and their associated magical energies to help you get a handle on what they contribute to the energy of your home. Being aware of these energies means you can actively incorporate them into your spiritual work and take advantage of their benefits.

Metals

There were seven main metals known to the ancients. Each was associated with a planet (which in turn had already been associated with a deity) and assigned a sympathetic set of associations and correspondences. The seven metals of the ancients were gold (associated with the sun), silver (the moon), quicksilver (Mercury), copper (Venus), iron (Mars), tin (Jupiter), and lead (Saturn). Many of these metals are still used in today's homes and are listed here with their associated energies.

Iron and Steel

Iron is one of the most common elements found on earth and is thought to be necessary to life in trace amounts for most living organisms. Cast iron, one of the most common forms of iron found in the kitchen, is made of iron, carbon, silicon, and trace amounts of manganese. Steel is another common form of iron, alloyed with carbon to strengthen and harden it, along with other trace elements such as tungsten.

Magically, iron is believed to deflect magic and psychic energy and increase physical strength, making it a common choice for making protective charms and talismans or for iron filings in amulet bags and gris-gris pouches. People of various cultures have carried nails, keys, and other iron-made items with them as protective and defensive talismans. Iron nails used to be hammered above doors and windows to prevent entry by evil spirits.

If you are looking for a way to incorporate iron into your magical or spiritual work and don't wish to use cookware or utensils, using a piece of hematite is an excellent alternative. Hematite is a pewter-colored metal used in magical work for grounding and protection. Lodestones, pieces of stone with iron in them that possess a magnetic charge, are also used in magical work to either draw certain energy toward them and the bearer or to deflect certain energies away. Either hematite or lodestones on your altar or shrine will lend their energies to your spiritual hearth. Alternatively, you can eat foods high in iron such as dried fruit, dark green vegetables, nuts, whole grains, and red meat, among others.

Iron and steel are used magically for defense, protection, grounding, strength, energy, willpower, and courage.

Copper

Copper is an excellent conductor, and cooking pots and pans are often made entirely or partially of this metal. Traditionally, copper is associated with Venus, the Roman goddess of love and beauty. It revitalizes, refreshes, is associated with healing, balances outgoing and incoming energies, and is also associated with attracting money. Just as copper is an electrical conductor, it also conducts magical energy. It is an excellent metal to have around the hearth and home, as it enhances energies such as harmony, abundance, and attraction of positive energy.

Magically copper can be used for work regarding kindness, fertility, peace, harmony, arts-related undertakings, and friendship.

Aluminum

One of the most abundant metals on earth, aluminum is naturally found in several stones such as garnets and staurolite. Aluminum is usually anodized for use in pots and pans. It is a very dense metal, despite its lightness.

As one of the more recent metals, it does not have as many magical associations with it as classical metals such as copper or iron do. Modern associations are travel, communication, and other subjects associated with mental activity. As aluminum is very resistant to corrosion, it may also be used to enhance staying power or permanency and to resist unbeneficial change.

Tin and Pewter

Tin is most often found in the form of pewter. Modern pewter is tin alloyed with antimony, but older pewter alloyed the tin with lead and copper. Used for making cups and plates and other housewares, pewter is also commonly used for small figurines and jewelry. (Interestingly, Mexican pewter is in fact made of aluminum alloyed with other metals, not tin.)

Magical associations for tin and pewter include business success, legal issues, wisdom, growth, success, healing, and abundance.

Porcelain, China, and Earthenware

These ceramic-based materials are all made from clay and kaolin clay bases with various other materials added to them to create certain effects. They are usually glazed to make them watertight. Clay is an earth-based material, and so these items carry the basic associations of abundance, stability, and fertility.

Glass

Glass is basically melted and fused silicon dioxide with various minerals added to provide stability. Pyrex contains boron; lead glass or crystal contains lead to increase light's refraction to cause a sparkling effect. Silicon dioxide is found naturally as sand or quartz, both also associated with the element of earth and therefore with the energies of stability and abundance. The quartz category covers many of the stones commonly used in New Age practice such as agate, jasper, and onyx, as well as the translucent stones commonly referred to as quartz. In general, quartz stones are associated with energy, healing, and protection, among others for particular stones.

The Ethics of Magic in the Kitchen

Cooking in itself is a creative activity. It's also one of the most common activities in the modern kitchen, and therefore is one of the most natural methods through which you can express your spirituality and practice your hearthcraft for the good of your family and home.

This brings up the issue of ethics. The subject of ethics was raised in Chapter 1 with the discussion about values and how they can help you define your home-based spirituality. Here we'll discuss the ethically sticky and confusing issue of cooking for others with spiritual and/or magical intent.

In modern religions such as Wicca, it is generally accepted that attempting to affect someone else through magical or other means without their knowledge or consent is an infringement upon their privacy and expression of free will, and that spells or rituals designed to change someone's status or outlook without their okay is a bad thing. There are other magic-based paths that do not operate under this particular moral restriction. Hearthcraft, however, is not specifically magic-based, nor is it a religion. It does not seek to deliberately alter an individual's position or status for the gain or benefit of the practitioner or even for the individual being affected. What hearthcraft does do, however, is take full advantage of the open-ended opportunity to generally pass along wishes for peace, health, and happiness.

How does this differ from attempting to manipulate someone with magic? Well, first of all, infusing your kitchen activity with positive energy through channeling Divine love via your spiritual hearth or inviting positive energy into your home isn't manipulating those who live in your home or who visit it as guests. If you prepare food with nonspecific love, then those who consume the food and that love benefit from it in their own way. The key thing to remember is that by serving food made with love, those who eat it have the opportunity to absorb the energy that is enhancing it along with the energy provided by the physical component of the meal. They do not automatically do so. Their personal energy has the choice to accept the loving energy in your food and home or not.

If you bake a cake for someone you like with the intent of creating a love-spell to make them fall in love with you, that classifies as manipulation and interference. If you make a cake for someone you like with the intent of baking the best cake you possibly can, with the hopes that the display of your culinary skill impresses them and perchance may contribute to their overall feelings of admiration for you, that qualifies as noninterference.

Perhaps this feels like splitting hairs. What it comes down to, however, is that you are not seeking to manipulate anyone by making food with love.

So how do you use spiritual or magical intent in the kitchen? Well, for a start, you can use rituals (and here the word *ritual* is used in the sense of short mental and spiritual preparations before you begin) to help improve your ability to cook. You can attract as much successful and encouraging energy from your hearth as possible and direct it into the food you prepare. You can use mindfulness (see Chapter 6) and invocations to improve your ability to plan, prepare, cook, and serve meals (see Chapter 10). And above all, you can cook mindfully, keeping the goal of caring for those who will consume your meal clearly in your mind. Chapter 9 looks at the relationship between food and spirituality in greater depth.

Kitchen Folklore

One of the fun things about doing research into home-based customs is discovering the traditions and folklore associated with domestic activity. Here's a series of domestic customs you can use to help enhance your awareness of the spiritual nature of your activity.

- Stir the contents of pots and bowls clockwise to attract positive energy, or stir counterclockwise to banish things. Use one or the other according to the needs of your home or family at the time.
- Pass items at the table in a clockwise direction to maintain harmonious energy there.
- If you wish to clear the house of negative energy, clean it beginning at the back door and travel through it room by room in a counterclockwise direction until you reach the back door again, then sweep or mop out the door and off the doorstep.

- To attract positive energy, clean items in a clockwise motion. This includes dusting, mopping, and scrubbing as well as wiping counters and washing dishes.
- Draw a spiritual symbol that has meaning to you (either cultural, religious, or designed by you) with salt water on the windows of your house and on the front and back doors. Paint these symbols with clear nail polish if you want something a little more permanent.
- If you wish to further connect your cooking to your spiritual hearth, draw a spiritual symbol on the inside of the pot or bowl before you use it. A stylized flame is a good basic image to use.
- Empower your laundry detergent for purification of any negative energy clinging to clothes. Water has a natural purification effect, but empowering the cleaning substances you use boosts that natural effect. Do the same for your household cleaners.
- Running out of salt is said to be bad luck for the prosperity of the home. Keep a small packet of salt somewhere to ensure there will always be salt in the house. (This may be one of the origins of the custom of bringing a bottle of wine, a loaf of bread, and a box of salt to a housewarming.)
- Hanging braids or wreaths of garlic, onions, or hot peppers will keep your kitchen free of negative energy. Compost them every fall and hang new ones. Never eat them!

- Hanging bunches of dried Indian corn attracts prosperity and abundance.
- Leave an onion or clove of garlic outside below the kitchen window to absorb any negative energy trying to enter the home. You may leave them around the doors to the house as well. Place new ones there every month, or more frequently if the old ones decay faster.

Traditional Kitchen Tools

The tools used by households a century ago are no longer the only tools at a hearth-based house witch's disposal! There are dozens of tools available in the kitchen now. This section briefly touches on traditional tools and proposes contemporary equivalents.

Apart from the cauldron, which was discussed in Chapter 4, there are a handful of other traditional tools that are or have been used in magical and spiritual work.

- **The Knife:** The knife is a symbol of air or fire, depending on which Western occult tradition you subscribe to, and in some paths it is commonly used in a symbolic fashion. The partner to this tool is the boline, a knife used for actual physical cutting and slicing in a ritual context for things such as herbs, carving wood, and so forth. The boline sometimes has a white handle or a curved blade, while the knife is generally dark-handled and has a straight blade with two edges. Sometimes it is sharpened, sometimes it is left dull to demonstrate that it is a metaphysical tool. Of course, the last thing you need is a knife in the kitchen that you can't use. As hearthcraft is practical, it makes more sense to recognize the spiritual associations of the knives you do use. Knives are generally associated with action, decisiveness, resolve, and confidence.

- **The Wand:** Another traditional tool is the wand. The wand is either a symbol of fire or air (depending on what your belief concerning the knife is, the wand is assigned to the other). Fairy tales feature fairies and sorceresses with magical wands that transform and enchant; tales of wizards and druids often feature staves. Both the wand and the staff are symbolic of the same thing. Staves tend to be associated with solidity and grounding as well, reflecting the world tree and the axis mundi found in shamanic societies. The obvious modern tool that parallels the wand is the wooden spoon, a tool of transformation and blending.

- **The Broom:** Another ubiquitous magical symbol is the broom. Like the staff, it symbolizes grounding, but it also symbolizes the spiritual flights taken seeking knowledge from other spirits and worlds. The broom is said to be a union of the female and male symbols of brush and staff, and as such was used in fertility ceremonies, festivals, and rituals, especially to encourage crops to grow. In more modern magical use, it is used to sweep the energy of a place clean of negativity. In this capacity it is sometimes termed a *besom* and is often kept apart from the everyday broom used to sweep up crumbs and dirt off the floor. In hearthcraft, as every act is a spiritual act, using the everyday broom is a magical act in and of itself. The floor and the energy get swept clean together.

Modern Appliances and Magic

This section is not necessarily advocating the use of appliances in magical or spiritual practice, but simply lists them and their alternate uses or energies as they currently exist in many kitchens. If you do not have some of them, you're not missing out on anything. That said, there are a lot of things in your kitchen that you take for granted, like the coffeepot, the kettle, and the microwave, and while they are not traditional tools, you may not have considered them as possibilities for contemporary magical tools. However, as hearthcraft is about practicality, there's no reason to avoid things you could be using in your daily practice. Why should only certain kitchen activities or tools be spiritual or creative? Why can't you employ electric fryers and stand mixers?

The main argument against using modern kitchen appliances for magic is that the use of electricity somehow disrupts or alters the magic. To each his or her own, but I have rarely found that the electricity running through the wires set inside the walls of my home affects the rituals or spiritual work I do within those walls. The second argument sometimes given is that the individual who objects to them feels that it is somehow cheating if an appliance is used. But again, hearthcraft is about practicality! There is no point to making more work for yourself by doing it "the old-fashioned way."

In a different light, however, if you wish to celebrate something by offering up the time and energy it requires to do a task without the aid of modern technology in the kitchen, more power to you. It can be a wonderful, meditative experience.

There is one caveat to using your everyday appliances for magical and spiritual purposes: you can't always use them again for cooking if you've used them to grind or blend something inedible. Take a small food processor or coffee grinder used to make incense, for example. No matter how much you scrub, essential oils and resin powder might not come out. If you intend to use small appliances such as these for magical and spiritual-related work, invest in a secondhand machine to devote to that purpose only, for the sake of health and safety.

At the very least, recognizing your appliances and kitchen tools as partners in your daily life provides you with yet another opportunity to take advantage of the energies of your environment. Being aware of what is around you and how you use the tools at your disposal allows you to remain more in control of your environment. Becoming familiar with specific energies further provides you with the opportunity to use them with awareness and precision, thereby enhancing your spiritual experience and broadening or deepening the complex web of energies that makes up your hearth and home.

Understanding that every tool you use possesses its own energy is the first step toward gaining a better understanding of how the energy of your kitchen is produced and affected.

How to begin? Well, a good way to start is by blessing each major appliance in your kitchen. This isn't quite as insane as it sounds. As human beings, we tend to project personalities onto machines because we relate better to things that we perceive as having identities. By recognizing the appliances as participants in your activities at hearth and in home, you formally acknowledge their energies. If you wish to go so far as giving them names, do so. Anything that gives the appliance more of a recognized presence in your kitchen will help.

Your appliances and how they work impact your life in ways you often don't recognize until you lose the use of them through a power failure or system failure of the individual machine. When this happens your reaction is usually a negative one, born of frustration, which is understandable. That negative reaction impacts the energy of your home, however, and it is regrettable if the only conscious response you demonstrate toward appliances and their uses is a negative one.

Take a look around your kitchen and make note of the appliances you use every day. The refrigerator is always on; the stove is at your disposal; the toaster, coffee maker, and microwave are almost omnipresent in today's kitchens. What if, when you used them, you consciously applied their energy in a positive fashion to the overall energy of your kitchen, your home, and your life?

By taking a moment to formally recognize an appliance, you are signaling to your mind and spirit that this appliance is a valued element of your everyday life—and you are signaling this to the energy of the appliance as well. This isn't the place to go into a long discourse about the validity of energy produced by machinery and technological devices as compared to the energy produced by organic and natural-sourced objects; suffice it to say that everything has an energy signature to it, and that energy affects the environment in which the object finds itself. The mechanical-based energy of a toaster oven may be a bit more difficult to grasp and incorporate into your conscious everyday use than the energy of herbs or other symbols, but it is a perfectly legitimate energy. Again, it seems somewhat self-defeating to ignore the modern tools at our disposal when we are seeking to create a spiritually, emotionally, and physically nourishing hearth-centered spiritual practice.

A good place to start is by formally recognizing the major players in your kitchen, the ones that sit on your counters and are used daily or several times each week. One way of doing this is by blessing them (see later in this chapter). Think of blessing the appliance as a way of initializing its energy in a positive manner and weaving it into the overall atmosphere of your hearth.

As an example, let's look at the stand mixer. I'm focusing on this instead of the oven because it's a very specific small appliance, whereas the stove and oven tend to be more central in the kitchen. Apart from using electricity, the stand mixer isn't much different from mixing and kneading bread the traditional way. However, it can also be argued that with less input from you, less hands-on activity, you're divorcing yourself further from the potential to imbue your resulting bread product with more magic and/or energy. When making bread for specific magical or spiritual purposes, yes, I make it entirely by hand. But for everyday bread, I use a machine, and by blessing the appliance itself and the ingredients as I place them in the bowl, I'm maximizing the potential for hearth magic on a daily basis. As a result of a physical condition I am slowly losing strength in my hands, and therefore I can see that in the near future I will need to use the machine for mixing and kneading even bread for ritual use, and when that happens I'll be fine with it because I recognize that it's the intent and the recognition of the machine itself as a participating element within my hearth and home practice that is key.

Your Cookbook

Another essential kitchen aid that you probably overlook when you think of tools is your cookbook or recipe file. This does not mean a published cookbook but rather the binder or folder of recipes you've collected over the years, with the notes scribbled to yourself in the margins or the back of the papers, photocopies and hastily handwritten scraps of paper, pages torn from magazines, recipes printed from websites, tattered recipe cards stained with vanilla extract and coffee and tomato paste. If you stuff these recipes inside the front cover of your main published cookbook or have them loose somewhere, treat yourself to a scrapbook or a sturdy three-ring binder and a set of transparent sheet protectors. The latter is ideal, because the sheet protectors can not only be wiped off when you stir the soup a bit too enthusiastically; you can also slip notes inside them.

Your cookbook is paralleled by a Book of Shadows or a grimoire in exclusively spiritual practices. A Book of Shadows is a place where you can note down things you've tried, changes to spells, records of rituals, recipes, and so forth. Your cookbook is another form of this. Arrange it in a way that makes sense to you. Generally recipe collections are organized by type of dish—appetizer, main dish, one-pot meals, beverages, desserts, and so forth—but if you have another method of organizing your recipes, by all means use it.

Keep a kitchen journal as well, one in which you can note down prayers, invocations, information, or nonfood recipes related to your spiritual practice.

Blessing Your Appliances

This is a simple and straightforward act that can be done on a regular basis to help maintain the positive charge to the appliance's energy, tie it into the harmonious energy of the kitchen, and keep it happy. No supplies are needed for this, although if you feel it necessary or preferable, you can use a small bowl or cup of plain water, or water with a pinch of salt added to it.

Note that this isn't a cleansing or a purification, simply a blessing. If you sense that it is required, do a purification before the blessing. You may feel the need to do a purification the first time you do this blessing and not again.

The following instructions use the refrigerator as an example. To perform the blessing on another appliance, simply replace the name and the purpose/use.

1. Stand before the appliance. Touch it with your hands and allow yourself to sense its energy by opening yourself to whatever feelings or sensations the appliance may raise in you. The appliance may "feel" hot, cold, active, passive, slow, fast, eager, aloof, or anything else.

2. When you feel that you have a sense of the appliance's energy and/or personality, say:

> *Refrigerator,*
> *Thank you for keeping our food fresh and cool.*
> *Thank you for being part of our lives.*
> *I bless you.*

3. If you wish, you can draw a symbol on it in plain water, water with a pinch of salt in it, or with a dry finger. The symbol can be anything you feel is appropriate. A good default symbol is a circle, representing harmony. Or perhaps you may wish to use something like a stylized flame to represent the energy of the hearth of the home.

If you have difficulty sensing the energy of the appliance, consider what each one does in the kitchen and consciously associate it with a similar energy. For example, ice cream is sweet and thus an ice-cream maker may be associated with friendship, harmony, and love. Why not try it with a stand mixer? It combines separate ingredients into one harmonious entity of dough, so perhaps you may associate it with community, harmony, and active work. Cake tins may symbolize pleasure, celebration, and so forth. Your teapot may represent health, love, support, comfort, and peace.

If you wish, you can do the same for the areas of your kitchen: breakfast nook, pantry, cupboard, and so forth. Don't overlook the contents of your kitchen cupboards. Cleaning supplies, china, dinnerware, and silverware are all easily blessed and/or empowered for harmony and other positive things such as health. Bless the entries into the kitchen, too, the doorways and arches or passages into the rest of the house.

On the Magical Nature of Everyday Items

As you have learned in this book, hearthcraft is a practical practice. Here is a small selection of modern kitchen appliances and utensils with comments upon their use in the modern kitchen and their impact on spiritual practice. Look at your major appliances, small countertop appliances, and other kitchen tools and utensils. What kind of energy do they carry? What sort of things do they symbolize for you? Here are some suggested associations to help you out if you can't pin down a definable energy.

- **Knife sharpener:** focus
- **Can opener:** removing barriers, moving past obstacles

- **Bread machine:** comfort, foundation, abundance
- **Coffee grinder:** focus, heightened awareness, energy
- **Handheld mixer, stand mixer:** gentle but firm blending of disparate thoughts or energies
- **Espresso machine:** intensity
- **Milk frother:** play, thought, lightheartedness
- **Mandoline:** evenness, precision
- **Slow cooker:** slow and steady union

Explore your kitchen cupboards and drawers, and see what you can assign to the utensils and small appliances you find.

Regular Purification of the Kitchen

Even with the best of intentions and the attempt to live a spiritually fulfilling life free of stress, unhelpful energy collects, and in general the positive atmosphere you strive to maintain can get a bit ragged. As the kitchen is so frequently used, it may require purification more often than other rooms in the house. A string of clumsiness in the kitchen or bad luck in cooking may mean a purification is in order. Remember, your hearth is sacred to begin with, and the need for purification does not mean it has become tainted in any way; it just means a bit of spiritual housecleaning is in order. Refer back to the purification information in Chapter 7 for ideas on how to purify the kitchen and your home in general.

Remember that any activity taking place in the kitchen contributes to the energy of the hearth. Likewise, any activity in the kitchen also benefits from the energy of the spiritual hearth. Doing crafts, homework, and other activities in the kitchen helps tie them into the energy that surrounds the home and can have a beneficial effect upon the results.

Keep Records

Keeping records is important not just in everyday life but for your magical activities as well. Keeping track of what you did and when you did it helps you plan and schedule your activity, as well as offering you the opportunity to review your past activity for insight. At its most basic, a journal can be a collection of ideas and notes about what goes right and wrong, or it can be a place to store the tidbits of home-related information you collect about spirituality or everyday life.

Your journal is the place to copy recipes, rituals, ceremonies, purifications, and any other specific spiritual activity you do. You can be as specific as you like, including notes about the weather, who else was in the house at the time, your impression and emotional state, and so forth. It's a place to record bits of information about deities or spirits that you research, the meditations you do, the offerings you make and how you feel they were received. You can make diary entries about how you feel, the connections you make, and your thoughts about your practice of home-based spirituality. You can paste in color swatches, clippings from magazines, or paint chips if you're planning to redecorate, and insert photographs of your house at different stages to record its evolution through the years. You can keep track of the dinner parties you host, writing down the menu, the guests invited, and the culinary successes (or failures!). You can press flowers or leaves from your garden in it. You can record poems or prayers in it. In short, it's a catchall for anything associated with your spiritual path, for ease of later reference.

You can use a blank notebook with lined or unlined pages or a three-ring binder. The binder allows your inserted pages to expand as necessary, whereas the bound notebook may not close properly after a lot of use. It works best to use something that is at least 8" × 10", to allow yourself room to record and draw and paste things in.

Chapter 9

The Spirituality of Food

FOOD AND FOOD-RELATED ACTIVITIES play a significant role in our lives, and yet other than foods associated with holidays, we rarely think of food as having a spiritual connection. Food is a very physical thing, and as such we often forget that it has a place within our spiritual lives as well. This chapter is divided into two parts. The first part looks at the relationship between food and spirituality. The second half focuses on simple hearth-based or hearth-associated dishes and recipes.

Think about Food

Recognizing the spiritual aspect of food is an informal act that you can perform to touch your spirituality on a daily basis. Here's an exercise that can reveal some interesting facts about your eating habits: for one week, keep a journal of what food you prepare and what you consume. Note down the following:

- The ingredients
- Total time spent assembling and cooking
- Time spent eating
- Where you ate it
- How much was eaten, and how much was left over
- If the leftovers were eaten the next day or in days following
- What spiritual practices you engaged in while you did any/all of the above (what prayers did you say, did you specifically add an ingredient or herb with a magical intent, did you leave an offering to a god or spirit, and if you did so, when?)

This collection of information can teach you a great deal about how much weight you give to various steps of the food preparation and consumption process.

The Energy of Food

When you handle something, part of your personal energy is transferred to it. Your base energy is affected by your emotional state, which acts as a lens or a filter through which your personal energy passes and is thereby affected by it. This is important to remember all the time (it's one of the reasons you're not supposed to handle sacred objects without being properly prepared), but it's particularly important to remember when you handle food.

The common saying is that you are what you eat, but it is also true to say that you eat what you are or, more precisely, who you were when you prepared your meal. And if you're eating a meal prepared by someone else, you're consuming some of their energy too. (This may make you look at eating out in a different way, especially if you do it a lot because you think you can't cook, or it seems inconvenient, or you don't enjoy your kitchen.)

The spiritual dimension of food and food-related activity nourishes the soul through the exchange of energy. Preparing and consuming food spiritually is an act of appreciation for the here and now. Consuming food spiritually can involve thinking about the food's sources, its connections, its associations to the season, its place in your life, and the impact its energy has on yours, among other things. The spiritual appreciation of food is subtle, but it nourishes and strengthens your connection to the spiritual aspect of the world around you.

Everyone eats. It's one of the basic physical needs. A personal spiritual connection to your food gives it another dimension beyond the basic physical relationship of fuel to consumer, however. The very least food can do is deliver the basic calorie package with its vitamins and nutrients to the consumer. It only makes sense to enhance it by handling it with awareness at every step of the process in order to maximize its spiritual potential. Why would you not want to provide the maximum amount of good the food could do for those to whom you serve it? Why would you not use food as a spiritual expression and mode of communication? Because your energy affects food at every stage of the process of preparation and consumption, it's important to be aware of your energy while you do it.

As touched on in Chapter 8, there are ethical issues that surround using food as an undeclared vehicle of change for people other than yourself; it may be interpreted as magical manipulation and a trespass upon someone's free will, without the subject's consent. This is a good rule to keep in mind. How you prepare and consume food has a spiritual impact upon you and those you feed.

Food does possess its own energy, and generally this will be the predominant energy it carries. The energy of every person who has handled it will add to it, however, modifying and shaping the innate energy to various extents. An offering of food to a deity is an offering of the food's energy, but it is also a sacrifice of the physical benefit that might be obtained from it. (Theoretically, the spiritual reward for the offering outweighs the sacrificed physical benefit!)

Food and the Seasons

In today's world, you can eat strawberries in January and cherries in November. We've forgotten that once upon a time people had to seize the opportunity to enjoy seasonal food within a limited time frame. As different fruits and vegetables became available, the changing of the seasons was reinforced in the mind of the community. The energies felt during the different seasons can also affect the energy of your spiritual heart and in your home, so paying attention to them is a good way to further nourish your spiritual hearth and keep your home a place of comfort and renewal.

You can explore the seasonal and spiritual aspects of food today by shopping regularly at a farmers' market. Week by week, the produce available will vary in supply and quality. By familiarizing yourself with what is available at different times of the year in your region, you can gain a better understanding of those energies and how they impact the energy of the food you prepare. Bring a selection of that seasonal produce home regularly and prepare those items, sensing their energies as you touch them and taste them.

Prepare Food with Awareness

Food is such a presence in everyday life that it's easy to forget it's a spiritual thing as well as a physical thing. By clearing the mind and focusing on each movement and action you make during the process of eating, you can gain a better understanding of the spiritual nourishment provided by food. On a practical level, this practice also relaxes the mind and body, which in turn facilitates the consumption and digestion of the food, as well as deepening your appreciation for the taste and texture.

Eating simply to keep yourself alive denies the spiritual aspect of the act. By eating with awareness, you create the opportunity for that spiritual connection to reemerge in your life. To add dimension to the spiritual aspect of your relationship with food and eating, try the following:

- When you plan a meal, think about the various sources and origins of the different foods that you intend to involve.
- Consider how seasonally available food reflects the energy of the turning year and how internalizing that energy by eating the food in turn affects you.
- Take the opportunity to prepare and eat seasonally available foods and write down how your relationship with the season's energy is affected.
- Take the time to prepare your food in a relaxed, aware, and focused manner.
- Do not multitask while eating; take the time to consume that food in a relaxed manner, savoring each bite and appreciating the energy.
- Try not to cook if you are angry, resentful, or afraid. The energy transfers to the food; the energy creates a less than supportive environment.
- Always sit down to eat. Honor the food and the people eating it by taking the time to sit and consume it.
- Before you begin to prepare food, take a moment to take a deep breath and exhale with awareness to bring yourself into the moment.
- To help you focus, bless the kitchen by lighting a candle as a representative of the sacred fire, itself a representation of the Goddess. Another alternative is to flick drops of water around the kitchen with your fingers to bless the space, if that works for you. You can put a pinch of salt in the water if you like.

Like other work in the kitchen, if your mind wanders when you set out to prepare food in a spiritual frame of mind or if you have difficulty focusing on the spiritual aspect, don't stress about it. Try touching or standing at your altar or shrine for a moment before preparing food to serve as a visual reminder that it is a spiritual act. Lighting candles on the table or saying grace or a blessing can remind everyone of the spiritual aspect of eating too. At the very least, being in a neutral or positive frame of mind is key to creating and consuming food that is spiritually as well as physically nourishing.

Honor the spiritual energy of the food you eat by acknowledging its presence and participation in your own spiritual practice. Look upon the food you prepare and consume as a way to interact with the natural flow of energy, and respect your time spent eating food as an essential element within your ongoing dialogue with your spirituality. Like other natural objects, food has a great deal to teach you about yourself and your relationship with the world around you. Eating and preparing food offers you the chance to touch nature and celebrate your spirituality on a daily basis, without taking extra formal action. By simply listening to what the energy of food has to say to you while you consume it with awareness, you can appreciate the flow of energy and the affirmation of life, and you can further expand your home-based spiritual practice.

If you are interested at all in cooking on an open hearth, be it in a fireplace or outdoors, an excellent source is William Rubel's *The Magic of Fire: Hearth Cooking: One Hundred Recipes for the Fireplace or Campfire.*

Recipes

The recipes in this chapter focus mainly on very traditional hearth-associated dishes. This is not meant to indicate that only traditional foods can function as spiritual meals or in ritual environments. Rather, traditional dishes tend to focus on very fundamental issues such as comfort and basic needs. This chapter will focus on two very basic foods that are and were easily made at the hearth: bread and stews/casseroles. These two kinds of dishes represent some of the very best things associated with the hearth: harmony, slow blending of flavor and disparate elements, warmth, nourishment, and ease of preparation.

Bread

Bread is one of the essential basic foods of the Western world and has been one for centuries.

Basic Traditional Bread Recipe

This recipe comes from my friend Janice, and she has given me permission to share it with you. It's a very straightforward and easy technique. Most bread is easy; it just seems overwhelming for beginners. If you have a bread machine, this is not the recipe for you. It's worth trying by hand to have the experience. This recipe makes one large loaf or two small loaves.

You will need:

• 2 cups warm water
• 2 tablespoons sugar (or honey)

- 1 tablespoon traditional yeast (not fast-rise or bread machine yeast)
- 2 cups whole-wheat flour
- ½ teaspoon salt
- White flour
- Olive or other cooking oil

1. Put 2 cups warm water in a large bowl (preferably glass or ceramic) and stir in the sugar or honey until dissolved.

2. Sprinkle the yeast into the water. Wait 5–10 minutes for the yeast to activate.

3. Mix in 2 cups whole-wheat flour. Stir until there are no big lumps. Now add more whole-wheat flour little by little, mixing in well, until your mixing spoon (preferably wood) will stand up on its own in the middle of the bowl for a couple of seconds before falling over. It should have a consistency like cake batter.

4. Set bowl in a warm (25–30°C or around 80°F is ideal) place to rise for at least 2 hours. You may cover it with a damp, smooth cloth or not, as you prefer.

5. Add salt. Mix in as much white flour as the dough will take, until it forms a ball and stops sticking to your hands.

6. Sprinkle table or countertop with flour. Knead for at least 5 minutes, adding flour as necessary to keep the dough "dry" and not sticky.

7. Thoroughly oil a loaf pan. Preheat oven to 375°F.

8. Form the dough into a loaf shape. Put it in the loaf pan bottom side up, then turn it over (this is a quick way to get most of the top of the loaf oiled). Brush any parts that are still dry

with a little more oil. (If making two small loaves, separate into two equal lumps, form into loaves, place in oiled pans.)

9. Set back in a warm place and allow to rise again. Within 45 minutes to 1 hour, you should have a full-sized loaf in the pan.

10. Bake 30–35 minutes.

11. Take the baked loaf out of the pan as soon as you can safely handle it, and cool it on a wire rack at least 30 minutes.

Basic Loaf Recipe for Bread Machines

Here's a basic bread recipe for the machine. This recipe calls for whole-wheat flour, but it works well with white all-purpose flour or a blend of the two in any proportion as well. The egg gives the bread a bit more stability, but it works just as well without it. If you don't use the egg, you may end up using a bit less flour.

This recipe makes about a 2½-pound loaf. If your machine makes a maximum loaf size of 2 pounds, cut off a third of the dough after the first rise and allow it to rise separately, and then bake it as a small round cottage loaf on a baking sheet. Alternatively, if your machine has a smaller capacity, cut down on the yeast by 1 teaspoon and the flour by about ½–1 cup (start off with 3 cups flour and add more as the dough mixes to make a nice smooth ball, then make a note of how much flour you used in total).

You will need:

- ¾ cup milk
- ¾ cup warm water
- 1 large egg (optional)

- 1½ tablespoons honey
- 1½ teaspoons salt
- 4 cups whole-wheat flour
- 1 tablespoon yeast

1. Put the ingredients into the pan in this order (or in the order directed by your machine manufacturer if it doesn't follow the basic liquids first/flour/yeast order).
2. Select the basic sandwich loaf setting and press start.

Basic Scones

Scones are like a cup of tea: they're easy to make, are comforting to eat, and are quick and easy to serve to unexpected guests or just to make for yourself on a morning when you need a touch of comfort. They make excellent morning snacks or afternoon break treats.

This recipe adapts well to the inclusion of raisins, currants, nuts with a pinch of cinnamon, or chopped dried fruit. Use about ½ a cup of whatever you're adding.

This recipe uses whole milk, but if you have a full or partly skimmed on hand, use that. If you use a lower-fat milk, add a bit of cream or a dollop of yogurt for richness. If you want a sweeter scone, use more honey to taste.

You will need:

- 2 cups whole-wheat flour, plus extra for hands and baking sheet
- 3 teaspoons baking powder
- ½ teaspoon salt
- ¼ cup margarine or unsalted butter (at room temperature)

- 1–2 tablespoons honey
- ¾ cup milk (whole, preferably)
- 1 large egg

1. Preheat oven to 4OO°F.
2. In a large bowl, whisk together the flour, baking powder, and salt.
3. With a pastry cutter or two forks, cut in the margarine or butter.
4. In a small bowl, mix the honey into the milk and add it to the flour and butter mixture.
5. Beat the egg lightly with a fork (try beating it in the bowl that held the milk and honey so as to blend in the last bit of honey sticking to the bottom) and add to the batter. Stir to combine.
6. Lightly flour the middle of a baking sheet. Scrape the batter onto the sheet. With lightly floured hands shape it into a rough disk.
7. Score the disk into eight wedges. Don't separate them; just cut the dough about halfway to three-quarters of the way through.
8. Bake 2O–25 minutes. Remove from oven and allow to cool 5 minutes on the baking sheet. Cut through the scores to fully separate the wedges. Serve warm with butter, jam, or clotted (Devonshire) cream.

These scones can also be made as individual scones. Instead of turning the dough out onto the baking sheet, flour a counter or pastry board and turn the batter out onto it. With floured hands, pat the dough down to about 1½" thick. Cut out individual scones using a round cutter (about 2½" across). When you press the cutter into the dough, do not twist it; the scones won't rise as high. Use a flat or offset spatula to lift the scones from the counter onto the baking sheet. Reroll dough lightly and continue cutting scones out until there isn't enough dough to fill the cutter. Roll the last bit of dough into a ball with your hands and pat it down to approximately the same height as the cut scones and place it on the sheet. Bake 18–20 minutes at 400°F, watching the scones carefully.

Focaccia

The word *focaccia* is derived from the Latin word *focus*, meaning "hearth or center of the home." In essence, then, focaccia is a hearth-bread. To the ancient Romans, *panis focacius* was a flat bread baked in the ashes of the hearth. You may know it as Italian flatbread, but many cultures have a version of it.

This is a basic version. It is extremely flexible and adaptable. If you have a favorite pizza dough recipe, you can use that, and indeed I use this as my pizza dough as well. I often split a third of it off to make focaccia and use the other two-thirds as a base for homemade pizza. It is best eaten directly out of the oven; it loses something of its personality if kept and eaten the next day.

This recipe uses half all-purpose flour and half whole-wheat flour, but you can use any combination you like. You can use a variety of toppings, including fresh minced onion, garlic, chopped olives, and sun-dried tomatoes; the only limit is your imagination. If you wish, you can knead the toppings into the dough itself instead; just remember to drizzle the top with the olive oil and sprinkle it with salt.

This recipe makes two focaccias or pizzas approximately 12" in diameter and is easily halved for a single focaccia.

You will need:

- ½ cup warm water
- 1 tablespoon honey
- 2 teaspoons yeast
- 2 cups flour plus 2½ cups
- 1½ teaspoons salt
- 2 tablespoons olive oil
- Warm water
- Cornmeal for dusting sheet

Toppings:

- Olive oil
- Kosher sea salt
- ½ cup freshly grated Parmesan cheese
- Parsley
- Basil
- Oregano

1. In a small bowl or cup, mix water and honey; sprinkle yeast on top. Allow to sit 8–10 minutes until yeast is foamy.
2. In a large bowl, whisk together 2 cups flour and the salt. Add yeast mixture and oil, and mix thoroughly.
3. Alternate adding warm water and as much of remaining flour as necessary while mixing, a bit at a time, until the dough forms a ball and pulls away from the walls of the bowl.

4. Turn dough out onto a floured surface and knead the rest of the flour in. Knead about 5 minutes until dough is smooth and elastic.

5. Lightly oil a clean bowl and place the dough in it, turning it to coat it with the oil. Cover it with a damp cloth and leave in a warm place to rise for 1 hour until double in size.

6. Preheat oven to 425°F.

7. Turn dough out and punch it down. Cut the dough in half and cover one half while you work with the other. Knead dough briefly and pat it into a rough circle about ¾" thick (or to your preferred thickness).

8. Lightly oil a baking sheet and sprinkle it with cornmeal. Move the dough circle to the sheet. Using your fingers, press indentations into the surface of the dough. Leave it to rise for approximately 20 minutes. If you prefer a flatter bread, put it directly in the oven.

9. Brush the surface of the dough with olive oil. Sprinkle it with coarse sea salt. Then sprinkle it with ¼ cup grated Parmesan cheese, and parsley, basil, and oregano to your taste. Repeat with the other focaccia.

10. Bake focaccia 20 minutes, or until golden. Allow to cool until it can be handled and slice into wedges.

Corn Bread

Another quick and very easy bread, this is wonderful served with stew or chili. This recipe can be made in a regular 8" × 8" square pan or a pie plate, but it can also be baked in a skillet or frying pan that is oven-safe. Why not try baking it in your cast-iron cauldron? Make sure your cauldron is big enough; an 8"-diameter pot is ideal.

You will need:

- Oil for greasing pan
- 1 large egg (beaten)
- 1 cup milk
- ¼ cup oil (vegetable or olive)
- 1 tablespoon sugar
- 2 cups yellow cornmeal (you may substitute up to half the amount of cornmeal with flour)

1. Heat oven to 425°F. Grease the inside of the pan and place it in the oven.
2. In a medium bowl, beat the egg and add the milk and oil. Stir in sugar, then cornmeal, just until moistened. The batter should be lumpy—do not overmix.
3. Carefully remove the pan from the oven and pour in the batter. Return the pan to the oven.
4. Bake 20–30 minutes or until the surface is golden brown and a knife inserted in the center comes out clean. Serve warm.

Stews and Casseroles

These are the ultimate one-dish meals. Hearth-associated foods tend to be easily put together and are often one-dish or one-pot affairs.

Beef Stew

You will notice the absence of potatoes in this recipe. While potatoes are traditionally included in beef stews, this one is served over a bowl of brown rice. If you wish to include potatoes, dice them and add them with the tomato sauce. Serves four.

You will need:

- Beef stew cubes (approximately 1½ pounds)
- ⅓ cup flour
- Salt, to taste
- Pepper, to taste
- 1 tablespoon olive oil
- 1 large onion, peeled and chopped
- 4–5 medium carrots, scraped and sliced
- 3 stalks celery, washed and chopped
- 1 clove garlic, finely minced
- ⅓ cup tomato sauce
- 1 cup beef stock
- ½ cup wine (either red or white)
- 2 bay leaves
- 1 teaspoon oregano
- 1 teaspoon basil
- Button mushrooms (optional)

1. Toss the beef cubes in a medium mixing bowl with the flour and salt and pepper.
2. Over medium heat, heat the olive oil in a large pot. Add onions, carrots, and celery. Fry until the chopped onion is

fragrant and soft, about 5–7 minutes. Add the garlic and stir-fry another minute.

3. Add a bit more olive oil if necessary. Add the floured beef cubes and stir continually, browning the meat.

4. Add the tomato sauce and keep stirring. Pour in the stock and the wine.

5. Add the bay leaves and the other herbs to taste. Add more salt and pepper if necessary. Add mushrooms if using.

6. Cover and reduce heat to minimum. Simmer at least 3 hours. Remove bay leaves before serving.

Hunter's Chicken

Also known as chicken cacciatore, this tomato–chicken stew is best served over egg noodles. I prefer to use chicken thighs as they have a richer taste, but chicken breasts may also be used. It serves three to four people.

You will need:

- Chicken thighs (approximately 2 pounds)
- $\frac{1}{3}$ cup flour
- Salt, to taste
- Pepper, to taste
- Fresh button mushrooms (or diced portobello mushrooms)
- 1 tablespoon olive oil
- 1 large onion, peeled and chopped
- 1 clove garlic, finely minced
- $\frac{1}{3}$ cup tomato sauce
- 1 cup chicken stock

- ½ cup wine (either red or white)
- 2 bay leaves
- 1 teaspoon oregano
- 1 teaspoon basil

1. Chop the chicken into pieces roughly 1" × 3"; toss in a large mixing bowl with the flour and salt and pepper.
2. Over medium heat, heat the olive oil in a large pot. Fry the chopped onion until fragrant and soft, about 5–7 minutes. Add the garlic and cook 1 more minute.
3. Add a bit more olive oil if necessary. Add the floured chicken and stir continually, browning the meat.
4. Add the tomato sauce and keep stirring. Pour in the stock and the wine.
5. Add the bay leaves and the other herbs to taste. Add mushrooms if using. Add more salt and pepper if necessary.
6. Cover and reduce heat to minimum. Simmer at least 1 hour. Remove bay leaves before serving.

Portobello Beef Chili

This is my favorite cold-weather one-pot dish. I suggest serving it with focaccia, but it goes well with any hearty bread or corn bread.

You will need:

- 4–6 large portobello mushrooms
- 1 cup red wine (or more to taste)
- 1 tablespoon olive oil
- 2 medium onions, peeled and sliced

- 2 pounds ground beef
- 2 (14.5-ounce) cans diced tomatoes
- 1 (6-ounce) can tomato paste
- 2 (15.5-ounce) cans red kidney beans (or 2 cans mixed beans)
- 2 bay leaves
- Chili powder or dried chilis, to taste
- Salt, to taste
- Pepper, to taste

1. Chop portobello mushrooms into small dice shapes, approximately ½" square, and place them in a medium mixing bowl. Pour the red wine over the mushrooms. Refrigerate and allow to marinate at least 2 hours. Stir occasionally to make sure all the mushrooms have been marinated in the wine.

2. In a large pot, heat olive oil over medium heat. Add sliced onions and fry until fragrant and soft, about 5–7 minutes.

3. Add ground beef and fry until browned. Spoon off any fat.

4. Add tomatoes and tomato paste. Stir.

5. Stir in beans.

6. Stir in mushrooms and red wine mixture. Add bay leaves. Add chili powder or chilis. Add salt and pepper to taste. Add more red wine if desired.

7. Reduce heat to minimum and simmer at least 3 hours.

8. Serve with warm focaccia. If desired, grated sharp or extra-old Cheddar may be sprinkled on top of each bowl of chili.

Chapter 10

Herbs, Crafts, and Other Hearth-Related Magic Work

SINCE THE HOUSE WITCH'S PATH REVOLVES around home and family, a chapter devoted to crafts and techniques through which hearth magic may be shared seems essential! This chapter explores basic techniques found in magical practice that are particularly suited to hearth magic, such as herbal magic. These activities and crafts are hearth-based in that they have as their goals the enhancement of your home environment and the health and happiness of your home.

The Magic of Herbs

When you page through herbal books, magical or otherwise, you will find that most plants are associated with protection and/or love in some way. There is a very simple reason for this: herbs and green things are reflections of the natural world, and these common associations are also two things most desired by humankind, knowingly or unknowingly. Both love and protection are two important themes in hearthcraft. Love doesn't necessarily mean for love spells or enticing someone to fall in love with you; this is a very common misconception. As a house witch, you want your home to be a place filled with love for family and friends. Love of the self is also important, as it signifies acceptance and support of oneself, something that is often rarer than it ought to be.

> If working with the energy of herbs interests you, take a look at my book *The Green Witch* for many ideas incorporating the energies of herbs and other items of the natural world into your spiritual and magical work.

To personalize your spiritual or magical activities, choose a signature herb or stone and add it to all your magical work. Enchant it with your personal energy first: hold and visualize your personal energy flowing from your heart down your arms to your hands, and picture it being absorbed by the herbs or stone.

Teas and Brews

The most basic way to make a tea is by steeping fresh or dried plant matter in very hot water, or infusing it. The resulting liquid is called an infusion. This method is most effective for leaves, flowers, and crushed fruit.

If the plant matter is chunky or dense, as bark, roots, or needles tend to be, then a decoction is called for. A decoction is made by actually boiling or heating the plant matter in water for a longer period of time.

> Warning! Make sure you know what you're doing if you plan on making something to drink. Use reliable reference books to identify and prepare herbal medicines or beverages.

For a longer-lasting liquid form, a tincture can be made. A tincture is generally also stronger than an infusion. It is made by infusing plant matter in a stable, long-lived base, such as alcohol or glycerin.

Here are some examples of basic infusions and decoctions.

- To make herbal or floral water, place approximately a double handful of your chosen plant matter in a sterilized covered bottle or jar. Pour boiling water over it until it just covers the plant matter. Cover with the lid, shake, and leave to cool and steep. Shake it two or three times weekly. After about ten days, strain and store the water in a clean jar or bottle. It will keep in the refrigerator for one to two weeks. If you wish to intensify the scent, steep a new batch of plant matter in the infusion. This can be used as a body splash or an additive for cleaning water. This also makes a very gentle space purifier when misted around a room.

- To make herbal vinegar, place a handful of your chosen plant matter in a clean jar with a lid. Pour vinegar over it until it just covers the plant matter. Leave the vinegar to steep in the refrigerator for one to three weeks. Strain the vinegar into a clean bottle and label it with the name and the date. Use herbal vinegar in place of regular vinegar or as an additive to wash water for floors or windows.

- To make herbal oils, place a handful of your chosen plant matter in a small saucepan and pour a cup of light olive or safflower oil over it. Heat the oil and plant matter gently over a low heat for fifteen minutes, then pour oil and plant matter into a clean jar. Cover the jar with a double layer of cheesecloth and fasten with a rubber band. Allow to sit in a sunny spot for ten days to two weeks, then strain oil into a clean bottle, cap, and label with the name and date. Use the oil in cooking (if the plant matter is edible) or to anoint objects, windows, doors, and so forth.

Here are a few other ways of using infusions and similar extracts:

- To make herbal or floral sprays, place a freshly made cooled infusion in a clean spray bottle and mist it into the air. Alternatively, place a few drops of a decoction or tincture into a bottle of clean water and shake to blend. It's not the amount that matters; it's the energy that the drops carry.

- To make floor washes, add an infusion, drops of decoction or tincture, or a few drops of essential oil to a bucket of clean water. Mop floor or dip a clean cloth into the wash water and wipe down walls, doorframes, window ledges, and so forth.
- For use in baths, add an infusion, decoction, or drops of tincture or oil to your bathwater.

Here are some suggestions for herbal blends that can be used for various applications such as simmering potpourri; sprinkling or sweeping powders; in sealed bottles as talismans; or steeped, strained, and used as anointing potions. If you can't stand the smell of one of these, or if you know your personal energy doesn't interact well with it, leave it out or find a substitute with a similar energy.

- **For productivity try:** cinnamon, clove, allspice, ginger
- **For healing try:** vervain, rose, chamomile
- **For relaxation try:** rose, chamomile, lavender
- **For communication try:** basil, carnation, lavender
- **For protection try:** vervain, rosemary, pinch of salt, clove

Potpourri

There are two kinds of potpourri: dry and wet (or simmering). Dry potpourri is about as simple as you can get: it's a blend of dried herbs, flowers, and spices placed in an open dish to scent the air and allow the energy to gently spread. Simmering potpourri is only marginally more challenging: the potpourri is placed in a pot of water and simmered on the stove. If you've ever mulled wine or apple cider, it's a similar process.

When making a batch of potpourri, it's a nice idea to set a small spoonful of it in a dish on your kitchen or hearth shrine as an offering. Dry potpourri also makes a good stuffing for herbal pillows, sachets, dolls, and so forth.

Basic Dry Potpourri Recipe

Don't chop up your plant material; if you begin with it fresh and intend to dry it yourself for your potpourri, try to keep the natural oils as unbruised as possible, as these are what give dried flowers and spices their scent. When dry, crumble the plant matter into large bits. The orris root is a fixative, something that will help fix the natural and added essential oils to preserve the scent of the mix longer. As a rule, use 2 tablespoons of the orris root powder per 1 cup of dry potpourri mix.

You will need:

- Dried herbs
- Dried flowers
- Dried spices
- Powdered orris root
- 6 drops essential oil per cup of dry mix

1. Place all the dried plant matter (including the powdered orris root) in a bowl and stir with your hands to combine. Sprinkle with the essential oil and stir again.
2. Keep the blend in a closed container for at least 2 weeks to mellow or ripen; this allows the scents to blend. Open the container and stir it once a day to keep it from going moldy. Even if you think your plant material is perfectly dry, there can sometimes be a drop or two of moisture left in it.
3. When it's ready, put your potpourri in an open container and place it in the area you wish to be affected by the energy.

It's important that you not forget about your dry potpourri once you've set it out. Dust collects in it, and exposure to air and the energy of the room will eventually weaken the energy of the herbal components. Make a new batch when you feel the energy of the old one has expired. You can bury used potpourri or compost it.

Potpourri Soap

One use for dry potpourri is as an additive for soap balls. It is easy to make this gently scented soap, as it uses grated soap bars as a base. Castile soap is olive oil–based and can be found in natural food stores or fair trade shops; if you can't find it, use a gentle soap such as Ivory or Dove instead.

You will need:

- 1 tablespoon dry potpourri
- 2 bars castile soap (or 1 cup soap flakes)
- Grater
- Microwave-safe container
- Boiling water (about $\frac{1}{8}$ cup)
- Chopstick
- 5 drops essential oil (optional)
- Rubber gloves
- Foil-lined tray or baking sheet

1. If the potpourri has large chunks, crush it into smaller pieces.
2. Grate the bars of soap into a microwave-safe container. Stir 1 spoonful boiling water into the soap flakes with the chopstick.
3. Microwave at 80 percent power for 10 seconds at a time until the mixture begins to melt and bubble. Remove and stir with the chopstick; if the mixture is too stiff to stick together, add another few drops of boiling water.
4. Add a spoonful of potpourri to the soap mixture and stir. If you wish, add a few drops of essential oil to soap and potpourri and stir again.

5. Put on the rubber gloves. Scoop up a small amount of the soap mixture with your fingers and roll or press it into a ball. Place each ball on the foil–lined tray or baking sheet to dry.

Simmering Potpourri

Simmering potpourri is a more active way of diffusing scent and energy into a space, although it is less permanent. It also adds moisture to the air, making it an excellent wintertime activity. Keep a small saucepan for potpourri use only and never use it for food preparation. Essential oils can linger on the finishes of pots and pans.

Dried apple slices and citrus peel make particularly good fixatives for simmering potpourri. Keep the peels from grapefruits or oranges and chop them into roughly 1"-square bits, or slice the apple into $\frac{1}{4}$"-thick slices. Allow these to dry, then sprinkle your choice of essential oil on them and place in a covered container. Open the container and stir daily until the peels or apple have absorbed the oils.

As a rule, use $\frac{1}{2}$ cup herbal blend to 2 cups water. Place both in a saucepan on the stove and gently simmer over low heat. Check it every quarter hour or so to make sure the water doesn't evaporate. Simply add more water as desired.

You can reuse simmering potpourri; simply drain the water from the pot and spread the plant matter out on a tea towel to dry or line a strainer with a tea towel and strain the contents of the pot into it, allowing the plant matter to dry there (spread it out as far as possible and stir it once or twice a day to keep the air circulating and aid in the drying process). Be aware that the plant matter may stain the towel, so use an old one or one made of dark-colored fabric. When the potpourri is dry, place it in a bowl or jar to be used the next time. Mark the container with the blend and its purpose. Potpourri that is made of powdered herbs, as you may have on your spice rack, cannot be dried and reused.

Alternatively, you can put the potpourri in a small muslin or unbleached cotton sachet and slip it into the water like an oversized tea bag, or you can use a pouch-style tea bag designed for home blends. You can even place the potpourri on a square of doubled cheesecloth, draw the corners up and gather the cheesecloth together around the plant matter, and tie it closed with plain kitchen string.

There are special potpourri-warming pots designed for simmering potpourri that resemble deep cups with a partially open chamber beneath for a candle, or ones that run on electric power like mini slow cookers. These are unnecessary if your kitchen is central enough to serve as the staging point for the scent infusion, but if you're looking to use simmering potpourri in a room far away from your kitchen, then you may wish to look into one of these options. Use sensible safety precautions with these devices and keep a close eye on the water level. Keep them very clean, too, to avoid flare-ups or cracking. If you have old-fashioned radiators, you can place a bowl on them instead and allow the heat of the water inside to warm the potpourri water. Be very careful if you use this open-bowl method and have children or pets.

Winter Holiday Simmering Potpourri

Here's a simple simmering potpourri to use during the winter holiday season.

You will need:

- 2 tablespoons ground cinnamon (or 2 large or 3 small cinnamon sticks)
- 1 tablespoon ground ginger
- 1 tablespoon whole cloves (or 1 teaspoon ground cloves)
- 1 tablespoon ground allspice
- 1 whole star anise blossom
- Dried lemon peel and/or dried orange peel (optional)
- Water

1. Place the spices in a medium saucepan. Fill the saucepan with water to an inch below the rim.
2. Gently heat the pot on the stovetop over low heat. Allow the water to simmer to release the scent into the air. Keep an eye on the water level; when it gets low, either refill with more water and continue to simmer, or remove from heat. Keep in mind that the scent will linger even after you've turned off the heat and taken the pot off the stove. How long it takes to dissipate depends on your house and how well the air circulates.

Sprinkling Powders

Sprinkling powders are used to distribute the energy of an herb or herbal blend around an area. It can be left permanently (for example, outside) or for a specific period of time and then swept or vacuumed up (if the intent is to absorb negative or unwanted energy).

Here's another use for sprinkling powder: rub a candle with oil (plain olive oil or a steeped oil of your own making), then roll it in a sprinkling powder to load up on energies associated with your offering/petition.

The easiest way to make a sprinkling powder is to completely powder a single herb or blend of herbs either in a blender, coffee grinder, or with a mortar and pestle, and sprinkle the mixture where you wish the energy to work. If you prefer, you can powder the herb(s) and then mix them into a neutral carrier such as cornstarch or baking soda. (Using talc is not recommended, because it can cause problems if inhaled.) If you use fine sawdust as a base instead, the resulting powder can be burned as an incense on a charcoal tablet (make sure the sawdust you use is safe to burn; sawdust collected from a workshop will generally be of wood treated with chemicals that are unsafe to burn and inhale).

Loose Incense

Making loose purifying incense is discussed in Chapter 7. Presented here is a set of basic instructions for making a resin and loose herb–based incense to burn on a charcoal tablet.

Herb and Resin Incense

You can use any combination of resins and plant matter, so long as you know they're safe to inhale when burned.

You will need:

- 1 part resin (combined or single resins)
- Mortar and pestle
- 1 part dried plant matter
- Small bottle or jar with lid

1. Place the resin(s) in the mortar. Gently crush the resin into small chips with the pestle. Transfer it to the jar. If there is any residue left in the mortar, scrape it out gently and add it to the jar.
2. Place the dried plant matter in the mortar. Grind into smaller pieces and transfer to the jar.
3. Cap the jar and gently shake it to combine all the ingredients. Label with the ingredients and/or name and date.

Incense Balls

Incense balls are a fun alternative to loose incense and are useful if you wish to include liquid ingredients. The basic ingredients are ground resins, powdered dry herbs, and a liquid (such as honey and/or wine). Easy to use, these little balls stay on the charcoal tablet, have little mess to clear away, and burn slowly to maintain a level, ongoing release of energy. They store well, too, and make good offerings at your shrine, even unburnt. The term *ball* itself can be misleading. In reality you will be making small chickpea- or bean-sized pellets. Anything larger will not burn properly.

Incense balls are burned on a charcoal tablet. Make sure you use charcoal marked for indoor use, often sold in religious or ethnic shops. Bamboo charcoal in particular is a good choice because it contains no saltpeter and is available in Asian markets or Chinatown areas. Never use barbecue charcoal, as the fumes can be toxic when concentrated inside.

If you prefer to make combustible incense—incense that can burn on its own—you will have to include a combustible ingredient such as fine sawdust, as well as another additive such as saltpeter (sodium nitrate or potassium nitrate) or ground charcoal, which contains saltpeter itself. If you are interested in trying your hand at this kind of incense, Scott Cunningham has recipes and instructions in his classic book *The Complete Book of Incense, Oils, & Brews*.

The basic proportions for making incense balls are:

- 1 cup loose incense blend (made of resins, woods, herbs, flowers)
- ½ cup dried chopped fruit (such as raisins, fruit peel, currants, apricots)

- 1 tablespoon honey
- Drizzle of oil or wine

Here is a list of suggested ingredients for incense balls. You don't have to use all of them; pick and choose from among those listed. Just remember to keep to a 1:1 proportion of resins to plant matter.

- **Resins:** Myrrh, frankincense, benzoin, copal.
- **Herbs:** Orris root, lavender, sandalwood, rose petals, cedar, cinnamon, nutmeg, bay, clove, ginger, rosemary.
- **Binding liquids:** Honey, raisins, wine, fruit such as apricots or currants.
- **Essential oils:** Optionally, you may wish to add a few drops of essential oil as well, either to enhance the scent of one of the herbs you are using or to complement it.

Incense Balls

Allow these balls to dry on a flat surface before transferring them to a closed jar to finish drying and to age. Putting wet balls in a jar can backfire, as the wet parts may grow mold or stick to one another and form one mass, making it difficult to remove a single ball to burn.

Here's a tip for making the task of crushing or powdering resins less of a challenge: freeze them for a quarter of an hour before crushing them. This makes them easier to powder. It also reduces the possibility of the heat of the friction melting the resin and sticking to the mortar and pestle.

You will need the following in the previously mentioned proportions:

- Resins of choice
- Mortar and pestle
- Mixing bowl (or coffee grinder)
- Herbs of choice
- Chopstick
- Binding liquid of choice (such as honey or wine; chopped fruits may also be added)
- Essential oils of choice (optional)
- Rubber gloves
- Waxed paper-lined tray or baking sheet
- Jar or bottle with lid

1. Crush the resins in the mortar with the pestle or grind them in a coffee grinder (kept for crafts only). They don't need to be powdered, only reduced to small chips. Remember, the heat from the friction of grinding them can melt the resins slightly and make them gummy. Empty the crushed resins into a mixing bowl.

2. Grind the dried herbs into small pieces and empty into the resin mixture. Stir with a chopstick to combine.

3. Mix in the chopped dried fruit, if using as part of the binding material. Drizzle the honey and wine over the mixture, followed by the essential oils, if you are using them. Stir to combine. The mixture should begin to clump together. Try forming a small ball; if the mixture falls apart, add more

honey or wine to moisten the mixture a bit more and test it again.

4. Put on the rubber gloves. Scoop up a bit of the mixture and form it into small pellets about the size of a chickpea or slightly larger. Set the balls on the waxed paper–lined tray to harden and leave to dry for at least 10 days to 2 weeks (depending on how much fruit or liquid you've used). Transfer the balls to a covered jar. Label the jar with the ingredients and/or name and date.

Sewing and Needlework

Needlework of any kind is a method of altering, changing, transforming, or reordering something, and as such makes an excellent basis for hearth-related magical work. Whether it's as simple as hemming new curtains or a tablecloth out of a rectangle of fabric, like any other craft sewing can enhance and deepen the energy of your home and spiritual hearth.

This section will not go into fancy needlework, but you will find one simple sleep pillow craft. If you're interested in other crafts that include sewing or needlework among them, look up Dorothy Morrison's *Magical Needlework* or Willow Polson's *Witch Crafts* and *The Crafty Witch*.

Herbal Sleep Pillows

Part of caring for one's family and home is making sure people get enough sleep in order to be well rested and able to operate at peak efficiency. If you or your little ones are having trouble sleeping, make a tiny sleep pillow to tuck under your full-sized pillow and encourage restful sleep. Dill and lavender are both associated with sleep.

Try using a thick material such as felt, otherwise the bits of dried dill can poke through the fabric. If you wish to use a particular thinner cloth, double it. The color or pattern are your choice, although try using a soft color instead of something vibrant or saturated.

You will need:

- Rectangle of cloth approximately 5" x 7"
- Needle and thread (a complementary or matching color thread)
- 1 handful dried dill
- 1 handful dried lavender
- 1 teaspoon dried powdered orris root
- Small bowl
- Straight pins

1. Fold the cloth in two, so that you have a smaller rectangle. If you are using a fabric with a right and wrong side, fold the right sides together. Sew along two of the open sides with a running stitch to create a pocket-like shape. Turn it inside out so that the seams are inside.

2. Combine the dill, the lavender, and the orris root powder in the bowl, and stir with your fingers to blend evenly.

3. Pour the herbal mixture into the pocket.

4. Fold the raw edges of the open side inside toward the herbal mixture. Pin the seam and sew it shut.

5. Tuck the pillow inside the pillowcase of the full-sized pillow. If it is for a young child, place the pillow on a shelf or hang it on a hook or nail on the wall by the bed, making sure it is out of physical reach.

Spell Bottles

A spell bottle is a collection of items with similar energy, brought together in one place for a specific purpose. Also called witch bottles, they're generally used for protection, but you can choose whatever theme you like. The bottle can be as temporary or permanent as you require. If permanent, you may wish to make it as attractive as possible in order to facilitate display on your shrine or the room it's designed to work in. You can even paint it a solid color or paint abstract designs on it.

The basic technique for spell bottles is simple. In a jar or bottle of any size appropriate to your purpose, add:

- Herbs that support your goal
- Stones that support your goal
- Coins
- Symbols (small figures made of clay or drawn on paper)
- Writing on paper (rolled up and tied with silk or cotton thread of an appropriate color)

Close the lid firmly, seal it with wax, if you wish, dripped from a candle. If you intend to keep the bottle in your home, decorate the bottle as you desire with decoupage, collage, painted symbols on the outside (runes, spiritual symbols, seals, or whatever you choose). You can varnish the bottle afterward to seal your art.

Some older recipes for spell bottles include pouring a liquid such as water or oil (for blessing or protective bottles), vinegar, or even urine into the bottle (usually for banishing bottles). This is not recommended if you're going to use the bottle inside or for display.

Spell Bottle Variation

If the spell bottle is to be permanent or a protective or enhancing talisman of some kind, try this variation.

1. In a craft store, look for clear glass ornaments. These are usually round and sold before Christmas. The metal caps slip off. Paint the globe first; it is very delicate, and if it breaks, you won't have lost all the careful work of filling it with your ingredients.

2. Take the cap off and fill the glass globe with your chosen ingredients. As the opening is so very small, you'll have to grind your herbs, use small chips of stones, and add very small scrolls of paper if you use them. The glass is very thin and fragile, so be careful. Use a funnel if you like or make one of a rolled–up piece of paper.

3. Seal the cap on this version of a spell bottle with a drop or two of glue to avoid the cap slipping off and the globe falling. Do not overfill the globe, or it will be too heavy.

These make lovely things to hang in windows and to give as gifts. They are especially suited to charms and talismans for abundance, peace, happiness, and health.

Spoken Magic

There is power in words. A spoken word moves air and creates the physical effect of sound waves hitting the eardrum. In this way spoken words bring ideas from the mental realm into the physical world, an excellent example of manifesting your will.

An incantation is a fancy word for a spoken piece of magic or the words that accompany a magical act. Other forms are charms, prayers, hymns, and so forth. "Magic words" are used in almost every culture's form of magic and also in worship.

Incorporating spoken magic into a daily spiritual practice isn't difficult at all. Spoken magic is a very common kind of practice. Think of saying, "Rain, rain, go away, come again another day, [name] wants to play" or "Star light, star bright" when first seeing a star. This kind of folk wisdom, speaking things in response to an event or occurrence, is rarely seen as a kind of magic. More often it's seen as averting bad fortune in some way or simply as habit.

Also known as "country sayings" or children's rhymes or even superstition, these bits of folk wisdom are sometimes rooted in actual historical events (such as the "Rain, rain" rhyme, which dates from Elizabethan times and is said to have originated from the storm during which the Spanish Armada was turned back from England's shores). They also can have a fortune-telling aspect, such as the "One for sorrow, two for joy" rhyme that can be applied to the number of crows or ravens seen in a flock or even to sneezes.

Alexander Carmichael's *Carmina Gadelica* is a collection of prayers, blessings, charms, and incantations from the Highlands of Scotland, gathered between 1855 and 1910.

Spoken magic is one of the easiest ways to incorporate spiritual or magical practice into your everyday routine. Choose certain times or events and compose short sayings or words to speak when they occur. Doing so offers you an opportunity to consciously reconnect with the spirituality of the day.

Keep your sayings and incantations simple. When you look at traditional sayings, they often have a beat or rhythm to them. Doing this with your own sayings facilitates the mnemonic. They don't absolutely need to rhyme, but a regular rhythm or beat does help. Keep the phrases short, so that you won't lose the rhythm of what you're doing and so they're easier to speak and remember. You don't have to declaim them; murmuring or whispering them under your breath is fine.

Here is a list of suggested times or events to initiate spoken magic. You don't have to use them all; these are suggestions only. Find a few that work for you.

- Turning on a stone element or oven
- Adding salt to a pot
- Stirring a pot
- Setting the table
- Serving food
- Sitting down to a meal (yes, saying grace!)
- Opening the kitchen door
- Sweeping
- Washing the dishes
- Wiping the counter
- Turning off the light at the end of the day

Here are some examples of phrases to help you create your own sayings:

- While stirring a pot: "May my life be as cared for as my cooking."
- While serving food: "May the food about to be eaten nourish my family in both body and soul."
- While sweeping: "May all negative and non-supportive energy be removed from this place."
- When turning off the kitchen light at night: "Bless this kitchen and keep those of us who use it safe and in health through the night."

• When opening the door: "May only health, love, and joy come through this door into this house."

Traditional incantations and charms tend to invoke a deity of some kind. As this book is not specifically linked to any one deity in any particular spiritual or religious practice, there are no deity-linked sayings included here. However, people often like to link their sayings to their deity of choice, and I encourage you to do the same if you feel drawn to doing so. It can be as simple as saying, "In the name of [deity]" before the rest of the incantation.

Corn Husk Doll

The craft of making a corn husk doll is often performed around the first harvest festival at the beginning of August (Lammas is celebrated in some English-speaking countries in the Northern Hemisphere, and Lughnasadh is a similar Gaelic festival). Sometimes these dolls are used as the kitchen witch icons and hung in the window or above the stove for good luck. If you wish to make one of these corn husk dolls yearly, you can burn or compost the old one that has watched over your kitchen throughout the previous year. Save your corn husks when you eat fresh corn in the late summer; lay them flat on a piece of newspaper for a couple of days, then collect them in a paper bag and store them somewhere cool and dry like the garage. To use, lay the dried husks in a shallow pan of water to soften them up a bit. Soaking the husks helps make them pliable, so they don't snap when you bend them. They don't need to be soaked for long; five to ten minutes should do it. These husks can also substitute for wheat stalks in many crafts, if you cut or tear them into narrower widths.

Making a Corn Husk Doll

You will need:

- Between 15–20 pieces yarn for hair (each about 12" long), color of your choice
- Dried corn husks soaked in water (trim to approximately 12" long)
- Tea towel or clean cloth
- Natural-colored cotton string
- Scissors
- 1 twig, about 5"–6" long and approximately ¼" in diameter

1. Gather the pieces of yarn and knot them together at one end. Take the husks out of the water they have been soaked in and pat the excess water off with the cloth.

2. Stack 4 husks on top of one another, aligning the long and short edges. Lay the yarn along the top of the husks, with the knot near the narrow end. Roll the layered husks around the yarn and tie the roll just above the knot with a piece of string. Tie it tightly, but not so tightly that it cracks the husks. Trim the ends of the string.

3. Fold the husks down over the knot to make the witch's head. Tie another piece of string around the husks at the neck. The yarn for the hair will now be revealed.

4. To make arms, roll a husk up tightly and tie a piece of string around the middle to keep it rolled. Slide the arm piece between the layers of folded-down husks. If you like you can tear the body husks a bit to place the arms where you want them. Trim the arms to the desired length and tie off each wrist area with a short piece of string.

5. Make the waist by tying a piece of string just below the arms.

6. To make a broom, cut a 1"-long piece from the wide end of a husk. Cut a fringe in this piece by snipping a series of lines into it, leaving a solid strip about ¼" deep. With the fringed end down, roll the strip around the end of the twig and tie it with a piece of string. Secure the broom to one of the hands by tying it with a piece of string.

Honoring the Seasons

This is a great craft that the whole family can engage in. It's particularly good for doing with small children. You can do one project each season or choose holidays throughout the year. When your collage is finished, pin it on the wall or tape it to the fridge. If you intend to make this an ongoing project, make sure you choose a location that can be more permanent.

Seasonal Collage

This collage can be made any size, but using the large 22" x 28" poster board size will provide plenty of space for images and found objects.

As an alternate approach, you can explore themes or ideas that are meaningful to you through a collaging project like this. It can be inspiring to explore aspects of your spirituality by creating an ancestor collage or a collage with the theme of harmony or the notion of the sacred flame.

You will need:

- Magazines, flyers, catalogs, old greeting cards, etc.
- Scissors
- Photographs
- Crayons, markers, colored pencils
- Blank drawing paper or construction paper
- Glue
- Poster board (color your choice)
- Found objects related to the season

1. From the catalogs, magazines, cards, and flyers cut out images associated with the season (e.g., summer-themed images may include beach balls, ice cream, sandals, sun hats, strawberries, sun, and so forth). Sort through the photographs and choose ones that support the theme of the collage, cutting portions of them out if you wish. Draw pictures or write words on the blank paper and cut them out as well.

2. Begin gluing the images and words on the poster board. You may lay the images out first to find a pattern that pleases you, or you can begin gluing the images wherever you are inspired to glue them and allow the collage to form on its own.

3. Attach found objects (twigs, small stones, grasses, shells, etc.) to the collage. This can be done as an ongoing activity, with found items being added throughout the season as they are discovered.

4. Take the collage down at the next holiday and begin a new
   seasonal collage. The past collages can be dated and kept as a
   record, although you may wish to store them in garbage bags
   to protect the found items (if used).

Creating Magical Figures and Symbols

This recipe creates a nonedible dough that you can use to make
small figures, symbols, and ornaments. If you intend to dry
and keep your creations, make sure they're not too thick or
large. This material is not designed for large-scale projects.

The basic dough is a neutral color, but you can color it by
adding drops of food coloring, powdered tempera paint, or a small
packet of drink crystals. It keeps well stored in self-sealing sandwich
bags in the fridge for anywhere between two and three months.

Dough Variations

There are several variations of the recipe for this dough found
online and in books of activities for children. Play with the
ingredient proportions until you find a variation you like. This
variation makes approximately 2 cups of dough.

You will need:

- 2 cups flour
- ¾ cup salt
- 2 tablespoons cream of tartar
- 2 cups water

- 1 tablespoon oil
- Food coloring or other coloring agent (optional)

1. In a medium saucepan over low heat, mix the dry ingredients.
2. In a measuring cup, mix the water and the oil. Add to the dry ingredients over low heat, stirring continually. Add the powdered coloring agent, if using.
3. Stir as the mixture thickens. Remove from heat when the mixture begins to pull away from the sides of the pot and forms a ball.
4. Allow the dough to cool. If you wish to color it with liquid or gel food coloring, separate the dough into as many colors as you intend to make and add a drop or two of the food coloring to each ball and knead it in.
5. To store the dough, seal it in zip-top plastic bags and press out as much air as possible. Store the bagged dough in the fridge. Allow it to come to room temperature before using it.

The creations you make out of this dough can be air-dried in a safe place; it will take approximately 1 week. Set them on a small square of waxed paper and leave them on a windowsill or on top of the fridge, turning them regularly. If you prefer to dry them in the oven, set them on a foil-lined baking sheet and bake them for at least 1 hour at approximately 250°F. Thicker objects may dry on the outside, and then the interiors may liquefy and run out of a crack, so heat them slowly. The resulting hard items will be fragile; handle them carefully. When dry, the objects may be painted and then varnished to help strengthen them.

Chapter 11

Spells and Rituals

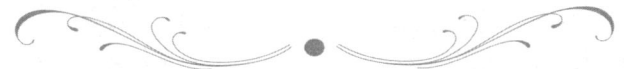

THIS CHAPTER IS A COLLECTION of home- and hearth-based spells and rituals, most of them using the symbols of the cauldron and the sacred flame in some way. Purifications and cleansings are also a main focus here, as a lot of home-based spiritual work consists of keeping the home energy as clear and as positive as possible to support and nurture the people who live in it.

Remember, in the context of hearthcraft the word *ritual* simply means something set apart as conscious spiritual work and done with mindfulness, nothing complicated or confusing. While they're presented simply here, you can make these rituals as formal as you like.

Lighting the Oil Lamp or Candle

This prayer focuses on the use of a candle or oil lamp as a symbol of the presence of Spirit. Say it as you light a candle or lamp.

> *Sacred flame,*
> *Burn brightly in my heart.*
> *I light this flame in recognition of your sanctity.*
> *Bless me, sacred flame,*
> *With your light.*

Consecrating Candles or Fuel

Hold your hands over the oil or candles and visualize the sacred flame represented by the hearth burning in your heart. Visualize the fire flowing from your heart to your arms and down to your hands. Visualize the light flowing from your hands to the candles or fuel, bathing them in the energy of the spiritual hearth. Say:

> *I dedicate these candles/this oil to the service of my spiritual hearth.*

Cauldron-Based Spells and Rites

Because the cauldron is a symbol of transformation, transmutation, wisdom, and abundance, it is easy to incorporate it into hearth-based spiritual work. Rather than repeat the rites already covered, the following will refresh your memory about the cauldron meditations and prayers in Chapter 4 and give you a couple to inspire you to create your own.

Cauldron Harmony Spell

When your home has been a little less than calm, or if family members have been having a rough time outside the home, kick up the rest and renewal aspects of the spiritual hearth with this little spell. This one incorporates both the cauldron and the flame as symbols.

You will need:

- Salt or sand (enough to fill the cauldron to the depth of about 1½", or more if the candle is tall)
- Cauldron (small one is fine)
- Pale blue candle
- Matches or lighter

1. Pour a layer of salt or sand in the bottom of the cauldron.
2. Place a pale blue candle in it. Light it, saying:

   My spiritual hearth is a place of rest and renewal.
   It nurtures me and those in my care.
   With this candle I invoke peace and harmony within this home.

3. Set the cauldron and candle on the physical analogue of your spiritual hearth or on your kitchen shrine.

Doorstep Cleansing

Here is an alternate and simpler ritual to cleanse your threshold or doorstep. It doesn't involve the extensive protection aspect of the Threshold Protection Ritual in Chapter 7, which makes it ideal to use on a regular basis.

Cleanse Your Doorstep Ritual

Vinegar is a great negativity buster, as is salt; cloves add a kick of purifying energy.

You will need:

- 1 cup water
- 1 tablespoon vinegar
- 1 tablespoon salt
- 3 whole cloves
- Bowl or bucket
- Washing cloth

1. Combine the water, vinegar, salt, and cloves in the container and leave to steep in a sunny place for at least 1 hour.
2. Dip the cloth in the liquid and wash the threshold or doorstep. As you do, visualize any negativity clinging to it dissipating. Say: *I hereby cleanse this threshold of negative energy.*
3. Repeat regularly and as necessary.

House Blessing

This is a full-length, multistep ritual to bless your home. It's basic and uses the four physical elements of earth, water, air, and fire to purify and bless the structure and the space. If you like, you may follow this house blessing with the Threshold Protection Ritual in Chapter 7.

House Blessing Ritual

You will need:

- Cleaning supplies
- Purification incense (see Chapter 7)
- Censer or heatproof bowl with sand
- Charcoal tablet (if using loose incense)
- Matches or lighter
- Candle and candleholder (color your choice)
- Small cup water
- Pinch salt

1. Repair whatever needs to be repaired in your house. Thoroughly clean walls, floors, windows, cupboards, stairs, and so forth. As you do, move counterclockwise through your house, finishing by sweeping dirt out the back door and shaking dust rags and emptying wash water out the back door as well.

2. Beginning at the physical analogue of your spiritual hearth, light purification incense (such as the loose mixture described in Chapter 7). Something like frankincense, sandalwood, or cedar would work well too if you prefer to use a purchased stick or cone.

3. Carry the incense clockwise through the house, going through each room. Don't forget to waft the smoke into cupboards and behind doors as well. As you do, say: *With fire and air I bless this home.*

4. Return to the hearth with the incense and replace it there.

5. Light the candle. Carry it clockwise through each room of the house as well, saying: *With light and flame I bless this house.*

6. Return the candle to the hearth.

7. Take the cup of water and add the salt to it. Carry it clockwise through each room of the house again. Dip your finger in the salt water and touch the outside of each doorframe, then the inside, and the frame of each window and cupboard, saying: *With water and salt I bless this house.* If you prefer, rather than simply touching your finger to the frame or door, you can draw a simple symbol that represents blessing to you. Return the water to the hearth.

8. Stand at your hearth and say: *Fire, water, air, and earth, bless my home and all those who dwell in it.*

Room Blessing

This ritual focuses on a single room and uses your associations with it as a basis for the blessing. As part of the blessing you will be creating a pouch to hang or place in the room. To prepare for this blessing, take some time to sit in the room you wish to bless and think about its identity. What color does the room's energy remind you of? Use this color to help key the blessing to the room. You can choose ribbon or cloth of this color for the bundle you'll be making. If you choose to use ribbon of this color, use white cloth; if you choose a colored cloth, use white ribbon. You may use a candle that is white or your chosen color.

You can further tailor this blessing to the room by choosing different stones or colors for their energies that you wish to introduce or emphasize in the room.

Room Blessing Ritual

You will need:

- Candle in candleholder (white or colored)
- Matches or lighter
- Pinch salt (for water)
- Small cup water
- Square of fabric 4" × 4" (white or colored)
- 1 small amethyst or clear quartz
- Pinch salt (for pouch)
- 1 penny or other coin
- Narrow ribbon approximately 10" long (white or colored)

1. Light the candle and place it in the center of the room. Say:

   By the light of this sacred flame,
   I bless this room.
   May it be a place of harmony.

2. Place the pinch of salt in the cup of water. Dip your finger in it and draw a line along the length of the threshold. Say:

   With this water and this salt,
   I bless the threshold of this room.
   May those who enter it know peace.

238 The House Witch

3. Take the square of cloth and place the stone, the pinch of salt, and the coin in it, saying:

> This stone for harmony,
> This salt for protection,
> This coin for abundance.

4. Gather up the corners of the cloth and tie it closed with the ribbon. Carefully pass the bundle above the flame of the candle, saying:

> I seal this blessing with fire.
> May this room always know light and love.

5. Hang the bundle above the door or place it somewhere in the room where its energy can continue to bless it and say:

> This room is blessed.

Personal Purification

This is a simple self-purification to do before an important act, or a good way to relax in the middle of something if you feel yourself beginning to get wound up, or if you're afraid or anxious about something. It makes a nice way to begin or end the day too. It's particularly helpful when you want to focus on something if your mind is wandering or won't concentrate on whatever task you're trying to perform.

Personal Purification Ritual

The candle you use can be one you light regularly in the kitchen as you work, or it can be one you keep for this particular purpose or for purifications in general. It does not need to be burned down completely.

You will need:

- Small candle (color your choice; white is always good)
- Matches or lighter
- Small bowl or dish of salt

1. Light the candle and set it on the table.
2. Place the bowl of salt on the table and sit down. Take the time to settle and fully feel yourself in the moment and be mindful of your actions.
3. Take a few cleansing breaths and lift your hands. Place your fingers in the bowl of salt.
4. Close your eyes and breathe deeply. As you exhale, visualize any negative energy or the undesired emotion flowing down your arms and out through your fingers, being absorbed by the salt.
5. Continue to do this as long as it takes to clear yourself of the unwanted energy or emotion.
6. Remove your fingers from the salt and open your eyes. Focus on the candle burning on the table. Breathe in, and as you do, visualize the warmth and brightness of the flame being drawn into your body, filling it with light and beauty.
7. Do this until you feel refreshed, focused, and calm. Extinguish the candle. Dispose of the salt by dissolving it in water and pouring it down the sink.

Creating Sacred Space

If you want to create sacred space in a more defined way for spiritual work, you can use this simple method. It's true that the home is in itself sacred space, but there are times when you may need to define an area that is set apart as particularly sacred for whatever reason. Think of this method as purifying a specific space so that it is immediately available for specific spiritual work.

Create Sacred Space

Here's a simple way to create sacred space. If moving around the space you wish to define is difficult, you can turn in place and raise the element to the four cardinal directions, visualizing the energy of the element flowing out from the symbol in your hands and pushing away any unwanted energy.

You will need:

- Candle in a candleholder
- Incense and a censer
- Matches or lighter
- Small cup of water
- Small dish of salt, sand, or earth

1. Light the candle and the incense. Take a minute to be fully mindful of the moment.
2. Carry the incense around the space in which you wish to work, saying:

   I bless this space with air.

3. Carry the candle around the space, saying:

   I bless this space with fire.

4. Carry the cup of water around the space, saying:

   I bless this space with water.

5. Carry the salt around the space, saying:

   I bless this space with earth.

6. Return to your starting place and close your eyes. Reach out with your heart and connect to your spiritual hearth. Say:

   I call upon the power of the spiritual hearth to bless this space.

Sacred space doesn't have to be dismissed or undone in any way when you are finished. The energy of the surrounding environment will gradually flow through it and return it to its everyday status.

Other Magical Recipes

Here's a collection of home-themed powders, oils, and incenses that can have various applications as you engage in spiritual activity in your home.

Carpet and Floor Purifying Powder

This powder features ingredients that clear negative energy as well as having the practical bonus of absorbing bad odors and refreshing your physical environment. You can also sprinkle it on fabric-covered furniture. It's nontoxic, so it's safe around pets.

Purifying Powder

You will need:

- ½ cup salt
- 2 tablespoons mint
- 1 tablespoon dried lemon peel
- 1 tablespoon lavender
- 1 tablespoon rosemary
- 1 teaspoon ground cloves
- Mortar and pestle or coffee grinder
- 1 cup baking soda

1. Grind the salt, mint, lemon peel, lavender, rosemary, and cloves with a mortar and pestle or in a coffee grinder reserved for arts and crafts use.
2. Combine the resulting powder with the baking soda.
3. Sprinkle the mixture over carpets and floors and allow it to rest for at least 2 hours, preferably overnight.
4. Vacuum or sweep it up. Discard the contents of the bag or dustpan outside.

Oil Blends

This book hasn't really addressed blending your own essential oils, because not everyone has the necessary ingredients at home. If you like to work with them or would like to try, here are some recipes for home-themed blends. Oil blends require a base or carrier oil such as grapeseed, sweet almond, jojoba, or other light oil. In a pinch light olive oil is fine. If you're sensitive to a particular oil, don't use it; substitute something else.

Try the recipes that follow. Tweak them as necessary to reflect the results you're looking for. Put a few drops of a blend on a vacuum bag when you put it in the vacuum. It makes the air smell great after a vacuuming session! The oils can also be rubbed on candles, used as anointing oil on objects or doorframes or even on yourself if you're in need of a pick-me-up.

Hearth Oil

This is a blend designed to represent the energy of an idealized hearth. It contains cinnamon oil, which can irritate, so be careful when blending it.

- 1 drop cinnamon oil
- 2 drops sandalwood oil
- 4 drops lavender oil
- 1 drop jasmine oil
- 1 drop rose oil
- 2 drops frankincense oil
- 1 drop pine oil
- 1 tablespoon carrier oil

Blend and bottle. Label with the ingredients and date.

Clean and Bright Oil

This oil has loads of cleansing energy. Add a few drops to the wash water when you're mopping the floor, or on a damp cloth when you wipe down the counters.

- 5 drops lemon oil
- 5 drops orange oil
- 2 drops peppermint oil
- 3 drops lavender oil
- 1 tablespoon carrier oil

Blend and bottle. Label with the ingredients and date.

Purification Oil

Use this oil to anoint objects in need of purification, or use it to cleanse stones or items you've been using to help maintain or balance the energy of a room. You can also put a drop or two on your wrists when you perform the Personal Purification Ritual (see earlier in this chapter).

- 5 drops frankincense oil
- 3 drops sandalwood oil
- 2 drops lemon oil
- 2 drops lavender oil
- 2 drops rose oil
- 1 tablespoon carrier oil

Blend and bottle. Label with the ingredients and date.

Blessing Oil

Use this oil to anoint objects when you want to bring a bit of positive Divine or spiritual hearth energy to them. This blend can be used in place of plain oil for the Ritual for Recognizing the Sanctity of the Hearth in Chapter 3.

- 4 drops sandalwood oil
- 4 drops rose oil
- 4 drops frankincense oil
- 1 tablespoon carrier oil

Blend and bottle. Label with the ingredients and date.

Sealing Oil

Use this oil to close off and protect areas or items. It's also used in the Threshold Protection Ritual in Chapter 7.

- 1 tablespoon carrier oil
- 3 pinches salt
- 1 whole clove
- 1 sage leaf

1. Combine all the ingredients in a bottle. Label with the ingredients, purpose, and date. Allow to sit in a sunny spot and infuse for at least 9 days before using.
2. To use, dip your finger in the oil and draw a line across or along the area you are sealing (around a doorframe or window frame, along a wall, across a threshold, etc.).

Incense Blends

Here are several recipes for various incense blends. Blend them according to the instructions in Chapter 7 (Loose Incense, Purifying Incense) and Chapter 10 (Herb and Resin Incense, Incense Balls).

Purification

Here's an alternate recipe to create a loose purification incense. I haven't provided exact measurements because beyond balancing one part of resin with one part dried plant matter, the proportions are up to you.

- Rosemary
- Sage
- Clove
- Frankincense resin
- Myrrh resin

Blend and bottle according to the directions in Chapter 7 (Loose Incense, Purifying Incense).

Ancestor Incense

Good for honoring the ancestors or appealing to them for aid and support.

- Rosemary
- Sage
- Myrrh resin

Blend and bottle according to the directions in Chapter 7 (Loose Incense, Purifying Incense).

Postscript

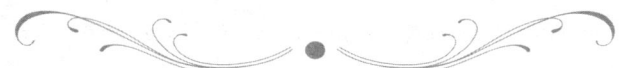

SEVERAL TIMES AS I WAS WRITING THIS BOOK, my thoughts moved faster than my fingers, and as a result "hearth fire" very often came out as "heartfire." I wonder, at times, if my subconscious was trying to tell me something.

At its core, hearthcraft is about honoring the home as a spiritual entity and a sacred place. The tips and techniques discussed in this book aren't what make a hearth sacred; it's how you live in a home that defines its sanctity, its ongoing life as a positive spiritual influence on those who live in it and visit it. In the end, your home-based spirituality is what you make of it.

I hope this book has helped you explore how you think of your home as a sacred place and has given you some ideas. It's by no means limited to what's in these pages, either; everyone's perception of the sacred is different, just as everyone's homes and practices are different. We seek and find sanctity and blessing in many different places. I wish you peace and joy on your path.

Appendix

Ingredients and Supplies

This is a brief list of the associated energies of herbs and kitchen supplies to use for various spiritual and magical purposes. It is by no means exhaustive. If you're looking for a good reference book to help you explore the energies associated with stones and plants, *Cunningham's Encyclopedia of Magical Herbs* and *Cunningham's Encyclopedia of Crystal, Gem, & Metal Magic* are good places to start.

- **Blessing:** olive oil, salt, water
- **Protection:** rosemary, salt, clove, angelica, bay, fennel, rue, sage
- **Joy:** lavender, lemon, orange
- **Love:** rose, basil, apple, cardamom, vanilla
- **Communication:** lavender, basil, carnation
- **Purification:** salt, fennel, rue, sage, lemon
- **Abundance:** basil, allspice, cinnamon, fenugreek seed, mint
- **Energy and action:** cinnamon, ginger, clove, chili peppers
- **Health:** ginger, lemon, apple, fenugreek seed, angelica, coriander, sage, orange
- **Meditation:** anise, frankincense, sandalwood
- **Purification:** angelica, sage, clove, salt, baking soda, lemon, rose

Basic Color Reference List

If a theme or energy you're looking for isn't on this list, think about the topic and choose the color that your intuition prompts you to pick. This is a good rule of thumb when looking at any color reference list: everyone is different, and one person's red may be another person's blue.

Colors

- **Red:** life, passion, action, energy, fire
- **Pink:** affection, friendship, caring
- **Orange:** success, speed, career, action, joy
- **Yellow:** intellectual matters, communication
- **Light green:** healing, wishes
- **Dark green:** prosperity, money, nature
- **Light blue:** truth, spirituality, tranquility, peace
- **Dark blue:** healing, justice
- **Violet:** mysticism, meditation, spirituality
- **Purple:** occult power, spirituality
- **Black:** protection, fertility, mystery, meditation, rebirth
- **Brown:** stability, home, career
- **White:** purity, psychic development, blessing
- **Gray:** calm, spirit work, gentle closure, neutralizing energy or situations

Bibliography

Ariana. *House Magic: The Good Witch's Guide to Bringing Grace to Your Space.* Berkeley, CA: Conari Press, 2001.

Carmichael, Alexander. *Carmina Gadelica Volume One.* The Sacred Text Archive. www.sacred-texts.com/neu/celt/cg1/index.htm (accessed November 23, 2007).

———. *Carmina Gadelica Volume Two.* The Sacred Text Archive. www .sacred-texts.com/neu/celt/cg2/index.htm (accessed November 23, 2007).

Clines, David J.A. "Sacred Space, Holy Places and Suchlike." Reprinted in *On the Way to the Postmodern: Old Testament Essays 1967–1998, Volume 2* (*Journal for the Study of the Old Testament, Supplement Series 292*; Sheffield, UK: Sheffield Academic Press, 1998).

Cunningham, Scott. *The Complete Book of Incense, Oils, & Brews.* St. Paul, MN: Llewellyn Publications, 1989.

———. *Cunningham's Encyclopedia of Crystal, Gem, & Metal Magic.* St. Paul, MN: Llewellyn Publications, 1998.

———. *Cunningham's Encyclopedia of Magical Herbs.* 2nd edition. St. Paul, MN: Llewellyn Publications, 2000.

———. *The Magical Household: Empower Your Home with Love, Protection, Health, and Happiness.* St. Paul, MN: Llewellyn Publications, 1987.

———. *Spell Crafts: Creating Magical Objects.* St. Paul, MN: Llewellyn Publications, 1999.

Dixon-Kennedy, Mike. *Celtic Myth & Legend: An A–Z of People and Places.* London, UK: Blandford, 1997.

Eliade, Mircea. *Patterns in Comparative Religion.* Translated by Rosemary Sheed. New York, NY: Meridian (New American Library), 1963.

———. *The Sacred and the Profane: The Nature of Religion.* Translated by Willard R. Trask. New York, NY: Harvest (Harcourt, Brace & Company), 1959.

Encyclopedia of Shinto. http://eos.kokugakuin.ac.jp/modules/xwords/entry
.php?entryID=208 (accessed February 22, 2008).

Frost, Seena B. *Soulcollage: An Intuitive Collage Process for Individuals and Groups.* Santa Cruz, CA: Hanford Mead Publishers, 2001.

Guirand, Felix, ed. *New Larousse Encyclopedia of Mythology.* 2nd edition. Translated by Richard Aldington and Delano Ames. London, UK: Hamlyn Publishing Group, 1968.

Homer. *The Homeric Hymns.* Perseus Digital Library. www.perseus.tufts
.edu/hopper/text?doc=Perseus:text:1999.01.0138 (accessed July 3, 2018).

Ingrassia, Michele. "How the Kitchen Evolved." Newsday.com, 2004. https://web.archive.org/web/20080408045613/www.newsday.com/ community/guide/lihistory/ny-historyhome-kitchen,0,2541588.story? coll=ny-lihistory-navigation (accessed April 8, 2008).

Kesten, Deborah. *Feeding the Body, Nourishing the Spirit: Essentials of Eating for Physical, Emotional, and Spiritual Well-Being.* Berkeley, CA: Conari Press, 1997.

Lawrence, Robert Means. *The Magic of the Horse-Shoe with Other Folk-Lore Notes.* Boston, MA: Houghton Mifflin & Co., 1898. www.sacred-texts.com/ etc/mhs/mhs00.htm (accessed February 8, 2008).

Lin, Derek. "Drink Water, Think of Source." www.taoism.net/ living/1999/199909.htm (accessed January 11, 2008).

Linn, Denise. *Altars: Bringing Sacred Shrines Into Your Everyday Life.* New York, NY: Ballantine Wellspring, 1999.

———. *Sacred Space: Clearing and Enhancing the Energy of Your Home.* New York, NY: Ballantine Wellspring, 1995.

McMann, Jean. *Altars and Icons: Sacred Spaces in Everyday Life.* San Francisco, CA: Chronicle Books, 1998.

Mickaharic, Draja. *Spiritual Cleansing: A Handbook of Psychic Protection.* York Beach, ME: Weiser, 1982.

Morrison, Dorothy. *Everyday Magic: Spells & Rituals for Modern Living.* St. Paul, MN: Llewellyn Publications, 1998.

———. *Magical Needlework.* St. Paul, MN: Llewellyn Publications, 2002.

Murphy-Hiscock, Arin. *Power Spellcraft for Life.* Avon, MA: Provenance Press, 2005.

———. *The Green Witch.* Avon, MA: Adams Media, 2017.

———. *Protection Spells.* Avon, MA: Adams Media, 2018.

Oxford University Press. *Shorter Oxford English Dictionary.* 5th edition. Oxford, UK: Oxford University Press, 2003.

Polson, Willow. *The Crafty Witch.* New York, NY: Citadel, 2007.

———. *Witch Crafts.* New York, NY: Citadel, 2002.

Rose, Carol. *Spirits, Fairies, Leprechauns, and Goblins: An Encyclopedia.* New York, NY: W.W. Norton & Company, 1996.

Ross, Alice. "What Is a Kitchen?" *Journal of Antiques and Collectibles*, May 2003. http://journalofantiques.com/2003/columns/hearth-to-hearth/hearth-to-hearth-what-is-a-kitchen/ (accessed July 3, 2018).

Rubel, William. *The Magic of Fire: Hearth Cooking: One Hundred Recipes for the Fireplace or Campfire.* Berkeley, CA: Ten Speed Press, 2002.

Telesco, Patricia. *A Kitchen Witch's Cookbook.* St. Paul, MN: Llewellyn Publications, 1994.

———. *Magick Made Easy.* San Francisco, CA: Harper Collins, 1999.

Thompson, Janet. *Magical Hearth: Home for the Modern Pagan.* York Beach, ME: Weiser, 1995.

Tresidor, Jack. *Dictionary of Symbols: An Illustrated Guide to Traditional Images, Icons, and Emblems.* San Francisco, CA: Chronicle Books, 1998.

Wylundt and Steven R. Smith. *Wylundt's Book of Incense: A Magical Primer.* York Beach, ME: Weiser, 1996.

Index